Printmaking: a medium for basic design

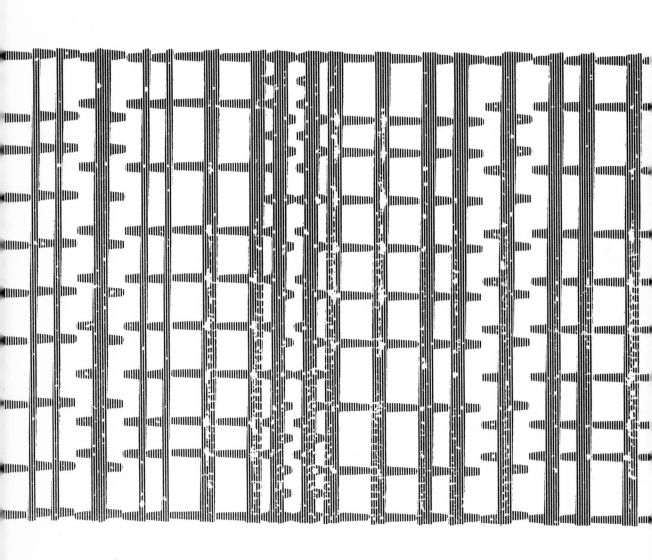

Printmaking
a medium for basic design

Peter Weaver

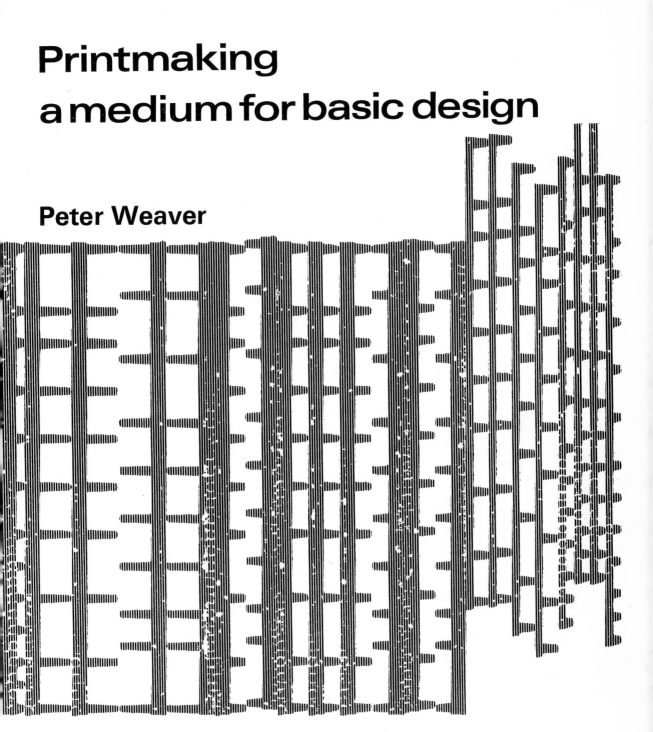

Studio Vista, London
Reinhold Book Corporation, New York
A subsidiary of Chapman-Reinhold, Inc.

For Felicity Rachel

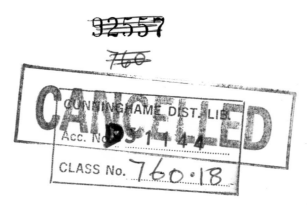

Acknowledgments

I should like to thank the many people who helped me by giving advice, making suggestions, or allowing me to reproduce work carried out by students under their supervision. My thanks are due particularly to A J B Sutherland, MA, Leonard Daniels, ARCA, T A Hartnup, J L Jones, H J A Crisp, Vernon Shearer, ARCA, John Astele, John Baird, Derik Redfern, Cyril Satorsky, ARCA and Trevor Allen. Also to the following students who worked on the more advanced projects: John Fisher, Keith Milow, Michael Gullick and Robert Woolner.

Finally I should like to thank Margaret F Bird who typed the manuscript and Jennifer Towndrow who edited and Gillian Greenwood who designed this book. PETER WEAVER

© Peter Weaver 1968
Published in Great Britain by Studio Vista Limited
Blue Star House, Highgate Hill, N 19
Published in the United States of America by
Reinhold Book Corporation, a subsidiary of Chapman-Reinhold, Inc.
430 Park Avenue, New York
Distributed in Canada by General Publishing Co Ltd
30 Lesmill Road, Don Mills, Toronto, Ontario
Library of Congress Catalog Card Number 68-16324
Set in 11 on 13 pt Plantin
Printed in Great Britain by W S Cowell Ltd
at the Butter Market, Ipswich
SBN: 289 37036 1

Contents

Foreword

Apart from outlining a course of basic design within the area that can be most usefully covered by print techniques, this book is intended to provide a source of ideas for experimental printmaking as applied to particular basic design problems, to suggest logical methods of approaching such problems, to define the areas of research susceptible to analysis through print techniques, and to indicate how the application of these techniques can deepen our understanding of the structure and order of the world we live in.

The print studio tends to be the one place in an art school where students from various departments meet and work side by side – the one place where students of graphic design, painting, ceramics, textile design, sculpture and so on can see each other at work, exchange ideas and actively break down the artificial barriers that so often divide these subjects from each other, and impede the free flow of creative ideas. It is a place where projects can be pursued that are framed to cut across such barriers. As basic design is an area of study common to all students, whether of fine art or applied, the print studio where they are all liable to meet becomes a logical place for the study of at least some aspects of this subject.* This development of a basic design-printmaking syndrome is of benefit to both studies, for printmaking studied in isolation tends towards a certain mannered technical specialization, whereas an involvement with basic design ensures its exposure to a wide spectrum of ideas and attitudes.

The value of basic design as a study is not confined to full-time students attending courses at well-equipped schools and colleges of art. It is a stimulating creative activity and an excellent discipline for the amateur artist working either in an evening institute or college of further education (often well equipped for printmaking) or at home without a press but merely a burnisher and an inking roller. It is also a study that enables the amateur to comprehend something of the creative thought processes behind much abstract art by actually experiencing similar methods of working.

*The problem of integrating basic design with the teaching programme as a whole is one that is becoming ever more acute, particularly as the teaching of this subject is becoming more and more widespread as the result of the introduction of the various new diplomas and in particular the Diploma in Art and Design and its related Foundation Courses. In the case of some Foundation Courses, basic design studies of one kind and another from the major part of the syllabus. Apart from the Dip AD, and various independent and County Council diplomas in such subjects as visual communication and environmental design, 'basic' design forms part of the syllabus in many vocational courses in schools and colleges of art, colleges of further education and art departments of universities, also in pre-foundation study in secondary schools.

In the USA basic design is studied in the Foundation Year in the BFA (Bachelor of Fine Arts) degree courses held by numerous art schools throughout the country. In liberal arts colleges and universities it would form part of the training for the arts major. The degree would most likely be a BA (Bachelor of Arts). In such an art major, it might be given in the second or third year, the first year given over to liberal arts subjects. It would also be an area of study preceding the 'fine art' courses (painting, sculpture, printmaking).

Introduction

One of the most dramatic ways in which printing can contribute to a greater understanding of the character of objects in the world around us is its ability to take an impression of the object itself, it being in the very nature of solid objects to leave impressions. Any hard object pressed against a soft surface will leave a record of that event. If we walk across soft ground we leave footprints; if we handle a book with dirty hands we leave fingerprints. Our knowledge of pre-history depends to a very large extent on the moulds left in the sedimentary layers of the earth's surface by the dissolving of original plant or animal material embedded in them. A great human disaster, the overwhelming of Pompeii by the eruption of Vesuvius, is recorded in all its horror and instant finality by casts of people engulfed by it left in the volcanic ash! By contrast with the record of an event that took place nearly two thousand years ago, a shadow is, in a sense, a print, a record, of an object – although a transitory one. The first prints made by man, knowingly and for a specific reason, were those of their own hands and fingers, dipped in pigment and pressed onto the walls of caves. The act of making a print directly from the surface of an object not specifically designed to be printed from is therefore not entirely new. Nor is it a unique or isolated phenomenon, for it exploits laws implicit in the mechanical structure of the world itself and gains significance from this.

To take a print directly from an object is a way of examining it, a way of exploring its surface, a method of research. So that at its very simplest, printing is of considerable value in a basic design context. However, the various techniques that are the basis of printmaking today, when applied to basic design problems, become potential tools for visual research. At the outset, in order to understand something of this potential, the fundamental techniques of printing must be considered and conclusions reached as to how they can be used. This is a matter of dividing printing into its component parts and examining their possible functions in this particular context.

There are four main methods of printing: *relief* which includes letterpress printing, line and halftone, lino cutting, wood engraving, relief etching etc.; *intaglio* which includes photogravure, drypoint, engraving, etching etc.; *lithography*, a planographic process; and *silk-screen* printing which is akin to stencil printing. Each of these techniques has its own characteristics and procedural methods, each its particular potentialities. Nevertheless, just as the divisions that have tended to exist between the various plastic and visual arts (barriers inimical to the free flow of ideas and development of new forms of expression) are now being destroyed, those that divide one print medium from another are also becoming blurred. This is reasonable, because in spite of certain obvious differences in the qualities of their end product, they are all of the same kind of technological organization. They all fulfil the same basic requirements; their differences in working method and consequent differences between the end product reflect the physical limitations of the branch of science and technology being exploited, be it mechanical, chemical or a combination of both.

It is necessary to be sensitive to, and also to react positively to these differences, but not to elevate them to an exclusive aesthetic. It is the technical procedures that print mediums have in common that are of primary importance in a basic design context. These facilitate the repetition of a particular image and make possible a whole series of controlled modifications and permutations of it by means of colour changes and re-registration. The use of such techniques enables the student or artist to produce the body of material, often necessary in experiments, in which a comparison between a number of related images is involved; and, in fact, to carry out a whole series of co-ordinated experiments into the nature and visual qualities of movement, pattern-making, modular systems and so on, without an undue expenditure of time and energy.

Firstly there is the ability to print a series of images identical in configuration but differing in colour tone and surface character and to print them on a wide range of different materials. For example, impressions can be taken from the same plate or block on a variety of surfaces and with many different inks:

a   In black ink on white paper (this would be the simplest most direct version) or on any other coloured paper, or metal foil-surfaced papers, acetate coloured or fluorescent or semi-transparent coloured glassine paper; or paper with different surface characteristics, from cast-coated art paper with its mirror-like smoothness to rough surfaced handmade paper.

b   Printed in various coloured inks.

c   Printed in various degrees of opacity.

d   Printed in various metallic inks or bronzed.

e   Printed in opaque ink on a dark coloured paper, producing a negative image.

f   Printed on transparent material such as acetate and viewed from the back in order to give a comparison between a right reading and wrong reading version of the image.

This aspect of printing technique alone provides a wide range of comparative material, so a single image can be modified endlessly and its expressive range explored. It is not only a matter of colour effects but also of surface character, qualities of the ink film density, thickness, opacity, transparency and light refractive characteristics. The differences between glossy ink on a matt paper, the texture of paper, both 'laid' and 'wove', can be contrasted with the glint of metallic ink or even the subtle almost tactile effect of metallic ink printed onto metal foil-surfaced paper. Ink and paper have a considerable range of surface texture reflecting their structure and their mode of manufacture. The extremely subtle textures that characterize ink result from the following factors and combinations of them (a) the pigment itself, the particles of which differ in size and shape, (b) the density of suspension of the pigment in the ink vehicle, (c) the thickness of the printed film of ink. Paper is made from a variety of materials, rag, wood, esparto grass, reduced to pulp by chemical or mechanical action, the sheet being made by hand or by machine, either 'laid' or 'wove', antique finish or calendered, cast-coated or transparent.

Secondly there is registration: this is the means used to ensure the correct relationship between successive plates in a colour print. From the basic design point of view correct relationship denotes any *predetermined* relationship between the plate, stencil, etc. and an image on the surface being printed on. Registration ceases to be an inert technical device and becomes a dynamic means of producing new images when considered in this way. It is particularly useful in creating an illusion or suggestion of movement of the kind found in stroboscopic photography. This effect is produced by repeating the image at intervals along a particular path determined by successive controlled re-registrations of it.

'Moiré' interference patterns can also be developed by a similar manipulation of an image. They are usually produced by superimposing regular geometric configurations (such as those in figures 12, 14, 15, 16 and 17) on each other at different angles. Evenly spaced arrangements of dots, parallel lines, systems of concentric circles and radiating lines can be used. 'Moiré' patterns can also be produced by superimposing regular geometric patterns onto relatively disordered ones (see plate 7). The configuration of a 'moiré' pattern is determined by the particular relationship between the two super-imposed images and its character can be very radically altered by even a very slight modification of this relationship. It is often the smallest movements of the superimposed image that produce the most startling transformations, and particularly those movements involving slight changes of angle. It is not usually possible to predict with any accuracy what form the configuration produced by combining two particular images will take, consequently the ability to print a number of variations is important, and satisfactory arrangements must be discovered by trial and error.

Reprinting in a modified register can also be used to distort an image (increase its width or depth) to produce the effect of a limited third dimension, to increase the density of areas of texture or pattern and so on. The combinatorial possibilities of controlled registration can be further extended by superimposing an inverted image, either on the same or a modified axis, by taking it through a series of 90° angles (this is best achieved with a square format). From such manipulations quite unexpected new images will grow, and it is a technique very useful in pattern-making. In the context of basic design it is the combinatorial and repetitive possibilities of print, the facility to make permutations and variations that are of such great value.

1 Exploring the character of found objects and artifacts

Taking a print directly from an object is a way of exploring certain of its physical characteristics; in particular its structure as revealed by its three-dimensional surface pattern. In some cases it brings to light a surface pattern more or less invisible to the eye (because of coloration or shallowness of relief) such as the pattern of loops and whorls in a fingerprint or the veins and structural ridges in a leaf. It may be a means of disentangling the three-dimensional element from the colour configuration of an object's surface; or a way of seeing an object anew, shorn of the colour usually associated with it. By reducing a number of dissimilar objects to the common denominator of black ink on white paper it provides a convenient means of comparing them in terms of scale and surface character.

A print taken from an object produces an image that at first appears to be identical to it, or at least a replica of a particular aspect of it. Certainly one can usually recognize the object it has been taken from and assume it is an accurate account of at least one aspect of it, and this is in a sense true. Nevertheless and paradoxically the print is also the opposite of the object, a mirror image of it, turning it from right to left or vice versa, laterally reversing it, to use the technical term for this curious phenomenon. In a mirror all asymmetrical objects are reversed; Lewis Carroll exploited this phenomenon and phenomena analogous to it in *Through the Looking Glass, and What Alice Found There*. Tweedledum and Tweedledee are mirror-image forms of each other, enantiomorphs. A cake is first handed round and after this it is cut into slices; time is reversed, the mirror image of an asymmetrical situation.

All organic substances are built of asymmetrical arrangements of atoms. Proteins (of which there are many thousands) are a basic element in living processes and are left-handed, asymmetry is basic to life. 'Symmetry, uniformity are the states of the dead world, they are passive, and, as it were, final. By contrast, life is active, disturbed and unfinished' (Dr J Bronowski).

Another method of taking images directly from an object is to make a rubbing of it. The image produced in this way although not laterally reversed is more often than not both opposite and identical to it, being a negative version of it (just as a hard object pressed into a soft surface leaves a negative version of itself). A rubbing records the configuration of the raised parts of the object in the form of a dark pattern on white paper; that is the part of the object which through weathering, light etc. tends in fact to be the lighter parts of it (this is also true of prints taken directly from the object). However, in spite of this inversion, rubbings of artifacts and botanical elements provide an image sufficiently accurate for use as reference material in museums for research. In spite of the paradoxes inherent in these apparently accurate methods of making a record of an object one aspect is truly recorded both by direct prints and rubbings and that is its scale.

TECHNICAL MEANS*

The simplest and most direct technique of printing is to roll up the object itself in ink, place it on the bed of a platen press and take a print. Objects suitable for such treatment must fulfil the following requirements:

a a reasonably flat surface with a clear relief pattern

b strong enough to withstand printing pressure

c movable and of a size convenient to place on the bed of a press.

This direct, relief, printing technique gives the sharpest, clearest, most immediate rendering of the surface character of the object. A similar technique can be employed in lithography. The object is inked up with a mixture of chalk-black proving ink and transfer or re-transfer ink, then either pressed directly onto a plate or stone or onto a piece of transfer paper, then transferred to a plate or stone.

The first method gives a rather 'open' image and is only possible with objects with a distinctly flat regular surface or slightly resilient surface. The impression having been printed or set-off onto the plate or stone is processed in the usual way. The second method gives a denser, clearer image, and objects with quite uneven surfaces can be used. Once the object has been rolled up in ink, it may either be pressed down onto a sheet of transfer paper laid on a soft backing (several sheets of newsprint or blotting paper) or the transfer paper can be pressed onto the object. This is a useful technique if the surface is curved. The transfer is then put down onto a plate or stone and processed using the gum-stencil method.

A similar technique in screen printing is to roll up the object in proofing ink, print it onto the screen, dust it with French chalk, then coat the screen with gum arabic (acacia) or shellac. When the coating is dry the ink can be washed out with turpentine, leaving a stencil.

Lithographic rubbings or frottage

The rubbings are made in the usual way except that yellow, white or buff everdamp transfer paper is substituted for detail paper; and soft lithographic chalk (Korns No. 1 or 2 are the best) is substituted for cobblers' heel-ball or other kinds of wax. The rubbing should be made rich and black to compensate for the slight loss of detail inevitable in transferring; it must be made on the coated side of the paper, in the case of yellow or buff everdamp papers on the yellow or buff side. The rubbing having been made, it is transferred to the plate or stone in the usual way (see Chapter 7, page 90); once on the plate the image can be worked into with litho chalks or litho ink, any weak parts made

*A resumé of technical procedures will be found in Chapter 7 'Methods of printing with and without a press'. In many cases alternative printing methods may be utilized to carry out an experiment depending on the facilities available at a particular school or studio.

good, and additions and erasures made. Processing is by the gum stencil method paying particular attention to the following operations:

   a After protecting the image with resin and French chalk apply a weak solution of gum-etch; this must be thoroughly rubbed down until quite dry, taking care that every part of the transferred image is finally left exposed.

   b Wash out the image (through the gum stencil) with a rich solution of asphaltum (wash-out solution) rubbing it well into the image. If the transfer is weak, it should be 'rubbed up' with developing ink or a mixture of asphaltum and chalk black proofing ink or transfer ink.

Roller impressions

This technique is a development of rubbing, substituting an inked roller for litho chalk. The objects from which the impression is to be taken are arranged on a flat surface and a sheet of everdamp transfer paper is placed coated side uppermost on them. A roller charged with chalk-black proofing ink mixed with transfer or re-transfer ink is taken over the paper at a pressure sufficient to deposit ink where the relief of the objects from which the impression is being taken, provides firm support. A large number of different effects can be obtained depending on the viscosity of the ink used, resilience of the roller and the degree of pressure exerted on the roller, quite apart from qualities intrinsic to the object from which the image is taken. For small objects or objects with complex or delicate detail, a small hand roller about two inches wide is useful, on simpler larger objects or collections of objects a wide litho pattern roller is probably best. The image produced on the transfer paper can be modified either by cutting parts out, pasting pieces of paper over the unwanted areas or by staging out with poster colour or gouache. Once transferred to the plate or stone, additions and erasures can be made in the usual way; processing is the same as for rubbings. Both techniques can be modified to suit screen printing; for example, a rubbing can be made directly on the screen.

Transfer collage

If the image is to be in the form of an assemblage of impressions taken from a variety of found objects and surfaces a collage technique can be used. First the necessary rubbings of various objects and surfaces are made on transfer paper in the way described. These impressions are then cut from the paper (they can be cut up to form new shapes) and arranged on a sheet of soft paper – newsprint is suitable. When a satisfactory arrangement has been made they are glued lightly in place with a water soluble paste, or stiff flour and water paste. The pasted up transfer is then put down onto a plate or stone and transferred in the usual way. Alternatively the impressions can be arranged face up on a sheet of paper, on the bed of a press. When a satisfactory arrangement has been achieved a litho plate is carefully placed face down over them and the bed taken through the press under fairly heavy pressure. The plate can then be turned face upwards with the impressions adhering to it and transferring proceeds in the usual way. The collage technique can be used in conjunction with any technique in which images are first made on transfer paper. It is a most flexible method of working because alterations can be made at almost any stage and one always has a fairly clear idea as to what the final image will look like.

Working method and experiments
Relief
In general the best results will be produced by rolling the object or objects up in fairly stiff black proofing ink (either letterpress or lithographic) and using a platen press for printing. If very thin objects or materials of even thickness are being printed from – wood veneers, embossed or perforated plastic or metal for example – a lithographic transfer press or an etching press can be used. If a litho transfer press is used, several sheets of paper plus a sheet of strawboard, hardboard or similar material must be used for backing to prevent the tympan becoming embossed. If an etching press is to be used (see Chapter 7, page 90), several sheets of paper and an old etching blanket or heavy felt should be used for backing. In both cases the press must be adjusted to suit the thickness of the material being printed from. Where no press is available or the object to be printed from is too large to put on a press, impressions can be taken by burnishing.

Where a number of objects are to be printed in relationship to one another, in order to emphasize their similarity or discordance or to make analogies etc., they can be arranged in the required configuration on the bed of the press and printed together, provided they are reasonably similar in thickness. Small differences of thickness can be compensated for by selective packing with pieces of card. Programmes of experiments can be based on such objectives as the contrasting of organic with mechanical surfaces, constructing tonal scales from surfaces of different tonality, comparing the back of objects with their fronts either by juxtaposition or overprinting or exploring three-dimensional relationships in solid objects.

Lithographic rubbings and transfer collage
Some points to remember when making a rubbing on transfer paper:
  a With a small soft brush remove any dirt or grit from the surface from which transfer is to be made.
  b Hold the transfer paper in place with weights or Sellotape (Scotch tape).
  c Keep the transfer paper in a plastic bag to protect it and prevent it becoming too dry.
  d If working outside keep the transfer paper away from the heat of the sun, otherwise it may dry out.
  e The rubbing must be made on the coated side.

Experiments based on brass rubbings

The initial experiments are concerned with exploring qualities inherent in the design of the 'brass' (or similar object) by printing it in various ways. The transformations caused by seeing it in negative or in a different colour enable one to understand something of the underlying principles of its design. It is a way of becoming familiar with an object, of seeing it in a new light.

a Print the image in black ink on white paper to reveal the primary image – the image expressed in its simplest and most direct printing terms (it will in fact give a negative image of the brass).

b Print on black paper in any colour, then 'bronze' in silver or gold. This will give a positive image of the brass. If dusted in gold bronzing powder the effect will be fairly close to the original in feeling and will have something of its dramatic splendour. An even richer effect, akin to the gilded backgrounds of icons or the gilding in medieval manuscripts can be produced by printing in vermilion ink on black or a deep richly coloured paper then dusting rather lightly in gold bronzing powder in such a way that some of the vermilion shows through.

c An offset of the rubbing can be put down onto another plate and the image drawn in solid with lithographic ink. This plate is then printed and 'bronzed' in gold; the plate with the rubbed image is printed on top in a dark-transparent grey. This gives the effect of the shiny metallic brass shining through its worn and pitted surface.

d Masking-out and re-masking techniques can be used to create a rich heraldic image in which various decorative elements such as the quarterings of the shield, the head-dress or supporting beasts can be picked out and enriched in strong colours.

Finally, probably the most exciting experiments are those in which a freer interpretation is attempted, experiments in which objects of the past are fused with those of the present, by the use of colour schemes inspired by pinball tables, motor cars or neon-tube advertising signs. Such effects can be produced by printing in coloured metallic inks or fluorescent colours on foil-coated papers or board, cast-coated art paper, glassine papers and so on, or by the introduction of 'foreign' elements into the composition such as gear wheels, lettering or devices from street signs or from labels, and emblems from motorcycles or domestic appliances. The serene knight lying so formally in his tomb becomes an astronaut or robot when overlaid with the searing colours and mechanical paraphernalia of today.

All the preceding experiments can be carried out just as well using as a basis rubbings from Aztec reliefs, the inscriptions invoking the blessing of Allah from Turkish cannons or similar objects, in place of a monumental 'brass'.

Roller impressions

Materials suitable for making impressions from can be gathered from scrap yards, car breakers, rubbish dumps and sites cleared for re-building. Impressions can be made from a number of objects, then arranged and glued down onto a backing sheet in the form of a collage. Or a number of objects could be arranged together on a flat surface and an impression taken from the whole assembly. It is a good idea to experiment with the effects of various arrangements on newsprint or similar cheap paper, to determine how heavy rolling should be and whether the required effect is being produced. Problems crop up when a number of objects of different thicknesses are to be used together. In such a situation the thinner objects can be packed up with cardboard, or some areas rolled over more heavily than others. Parts of the background will inevitably be picked up, and where there are sudden changes in the level of relief the paper will tend to crease and form fantastic patterns (plate 2). These effects are an essential part of the dramatic character of this technique and they should be exploited rather than avoided. They often give an overall unity to an image composed of very diverse elements and in some cases produce a complete metamorphosis in which objects of an uncompromisingly mechanical character become blurred and pitted, with strange seaweed-like growths springing from their edges; the mechanistic assembly becoming overlaid by a web of organic chance happenings, the rational and irrational becoming completely and irrevocably interwoven.

Fabricated surfaces
So far, in this section, we have dealt only with ready-made or found objects of one kind and another; it is, however, possible to make surfaces or pictorial elements which are designed specifically for making rubbings or rolled impressions. It will be appreciated that this method of working differs in one very important respect from the technique just described. The artist has complete control not only of the overall configuration of the image but also of the pictorial elements from which it is to be composed.

Suitable materials to construct such a relief surface are cardboard of various thicknesses, paper, thin sheets of balsa wood and of expanded polystyrene. These materials can be cut to the required shapes and their surfaces developed and enriched by scraping and scoring or they can be embossed by hammering or pressing into them (with a platen or nipping press) pieces of wire, washers, or other small hard objects. Layers of cardboard and paper of various degrees of roughness or smoothness can be glued together. To form thin lines or more organic effects, pieces of cotton, thin string, tape or bandages can be incorporated. The elements thus produced can finally be assembled for making rubbings or 'roller impressions' in various ways.

    a The elements can merely be arranged on a flat surface and the rubbing made.
    b They can be arranged on a sheet of hardboard or thick cardboard and glued into place and a rubbing made of the whole assembly.
    c Rubbings can be made separately from each element, cut up and assembled as a

collage. Using this method it is possible to combine specially made elements with found objects in one composition.

Owing to the fineness of detail and the relatively shallow relief of surfaces made in this way they tend to be rather more suitable for taking rubbings from than for making 'roller impressions'. If the image is built up from hard materials such as cardboard and paper (rather than balsa wood or expanded polystyrene which are easily compressed) it can be used as the basis for an uninked relief print (see below).

Printing method for uninked relief prints

a Place the relief block on the bed of a platen press, lay a thin sheet of 'polythene' over it. This is to prevent the damped paper from sticking to the block.

b Damp a piece of thick soft paper such as J Barcham Green Crisbrook 140 lb or duplicator board and place it in position over the block.

c For backing use a piece of thick felt (the kind used under carpets is quite good) and over this a piece of hardboard or millboard.

d Adjust press, using heavy pressure.

e Interleave the prints with newsprint or dry blotting paper and leave between boards to dry-out.

Uninked relief prints can also be taken using an etching press, a lithographic transfer press, a fly press or bookbinder's press.

Experiments with Three-Dimensional Objects

The object of this experiment is to give two-dimensional expression to a three-dimensional structure. For the purposes of the experiment a small wooden box or crate is convenient. This can be broken down into its component parts, sides, top and base, and these parts printed in relationship to each other in accordance with a predetermined rational order.

a Printing from the insides of the panels of the crate. Print the base in the centre with the four side panels arranged round it as if folded down, their bottom edges adjacent to the corresponding edges of the base, see figure 1.

b The same arrangement but printing from the outsides of the panels.

c The sides, either inside or out, arranged with their vertical edges adjacent to each other and in their correct order, see figure 2.

d Starting with the outside of one of the vertical panels, print it, then print the top edge in relationship to it, followed in order by the inside, the inside of the base, the inside of the opposite panel and so on until the base of the panel first printed has been reached. It is rather like turning the whole thing inside out, or skinning an animal, see figure 3.

The various panels can be arranged in accordance with standard architectural drawing

16

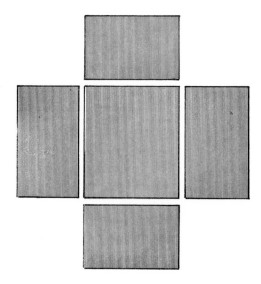

FIG I

FIG 2

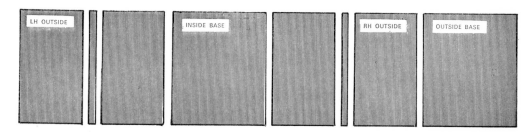

FIG 3

FIGS 1–3   Relationship between component parts of a box

practice, with plan and elevations rationally related to each other. Similar experiments can be carried out with any printable geometric object such as three- or four-sided pyramids, prisms etc. In plate 2 a Japanese puzzle has been subjected to this kind of analysis. Such analysis of solids (they are solids with developable surfaces and can be made simply by cutting and folding flat material such as paper or sheet metal) gives an insight into such subjects as carton and furniture design (disposable furniture is now made from folded cardboard). The same sort of analysis can be applied to structural design, space frame roofs, folded slab construction, and into three-dimensional structures in general.

B

2 Modular systems of proportion

At the very outset, as soon as the first tentative decisions are made – about format and configuration of a painting, print or piece of graphic design, decisions about its height and width, the primary divisions of the surface, the placing of pictorial elements within this framework – one is concerned with proportion. From among the many ways of approaching this problem, we are concerned here with those which involve what might be termed 'rational systems of proportion', systems of proportions that are based on arithmetic or geometric laws and on systems of standard measurement. A system of proportions usually consists of two integrated and complementary elements: a 'module', the standard unit of length or volume to be used throughout the design or structure, and a series of proportional relationships with which to generate a series of co-ordinated dimensions.

The module

A module may be based on any existing standardized system of measurement, such as the inch or the metre, any existing structural organization such as type, with its points systems of measurement (Anglo-American or the Continental Didot), or it may be based on a unit derived from nature, as for example the average height of a man, which is the basis of Le Corbusier's 'Modulor', and the basis of many systems of proportion in the past. The whole of nature is modular; its module, the brick from which it is built, is the atom and it is through this order, this structural regularity, imposed by the modular atom that we are able to comprehend it in all its diversity and complexity. 'The whole of our world, radiant energy and protean matter, crystals and cells, stars and atoms – all is built of modules, whose identity and simplicity belie the unmatched diversity of man and nature' (Philip Morrison). The list of man-made modular systems is endless, it is the basis of written language, the letter, the word, the sentence, the structure of buildings, in particular prefabricated structures such as Joseph Paxton's Crystal Palace in the nineteenth century and Buckminster Fuller's geodesic domes of today. It is the basis of all industrial mass-production and in particular computerized automated industrial production. The half-tone plates in this book, both colour and black and white, are examples of the end product of a modular based photo-mechanical industrial process; the module in this instance being a dot (examine the plates through a strong magnifying glass). Similarly the image on a television screen is composed of modular lines.

Proportional relationships

Probably the best known and most widely used number sequence on which systems of proportion can be based is the Fibonacci sequence. In this sequence of numbers (or dimensions) each term in the sequence is the sum of the two terms which immediately precede it ($21 + 34 = 55$); starting with 1 the whole series can be built up by addition – $1:1:2:3:5:8:13:21:34:55:89:144:233:$ and so on. There are a number of reasons why this particular sequence seems significant to artists and architects. Firstly, it is closely related to the 'golden section' or 'golden mean' of the ancient Greeks, a geometric relationship based on the ratio of 1·618 to 1. This ratio approximates to the ratio of successive terms of a Fibonacci sequence. It is, in conjunction with a module of six feet (72 inches or 182·9 cm.), the basis of Le Corbusier's 'modulor'. Secondly, just as modular design gains significance from the modular nature of the world and the universe, so the Fibonacci sequence gains significance by its appearance in nature as a means of organizing matter. It is to be found in the relationships of successive generations in the genealogical tree of the male bee, in the structure of flowers, the number of petals and florets in various orders, the branching of new shoots from the axil and also and more subtly in the exponential law of growth, its continual measurable quantities such as height, length and velocity. An example of the appearance of intervals in a Fibonacci sequence in nature is in the pattern made by the intersections of spirals of florets in a sunflower; these conform to two adjacent numbers in the sequence in that there are 21 right-hand spirals and 34 left-hand spirals.

Other number sequences

There are several number sequences that may be used as a basis for a system of proportions such as sequences based on number patterns, squared numbers, and logarithmic sequences.

Number patterns

These series of numbers are arrived at by arranging dots, representing a number, in a rational pattern. The simplest series of such patterns gives odd and even numbers, but the series most likely to be of use are generated from a square or triangular arrangement.

Square numbers are those in which the number is arranged as a group in which the number of rows of dots is equal to the number of columns.

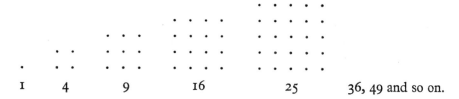

| 1 | 4 | 9 | 16 | 25 | 36, 49 and so on. |

Triangular numbers are those in which the dots can be arranged in a triangle.

| 1 | 3 | 6 | 10 | 15 | 21, 28 and so on. |

SQUARE NUMBERS   TRIANGULAR NUMBERS   FIBONACCI SEQUENCE   LOGARITHMIC SEQUENCE

FIG 4 Comparison of proportional sequences

Squared numbers

This sequence is obtained by multiplying each successive number by itself.
$1\times1 : 2\times2 : 3\times3 : 4\times4$ and so on, giving a sequence 1:4:9:16:25:36:49: and so on.

Logarithmic sequences

Logarithmic sequences are geometric sequences in which the sequence is built up by successive multiplications by a number which characterizes the sequence and which is called the common ratio of the sequence. $2 \times 2 = 4$ etc. 2:4:8:16:32:64:128:256 and so on. Common ratio 2.

A module system

It will be appreciated that in a structure based on arithmetic or geometric systems of proportion, accuracy is of the greatest importance, and that in a structure based on the varied multiplications and arrangements of a basic module, flexibility is also very important. A system meeting these conditions exists in the form of type, which by its essentially modular nature (as a tool to print language, which is itself modular) and by its precision (accurate fit to suit machine production) fulfils these requirements and provides a tool well suited to experiments in module design.

In this particular use of the 'typographical system', only certain type units are of value; it is in fact important to keep the number used to a minimum. Firstly there are the pictorial elements of the design, the units to be printed from. Of those available, rectangular border units and rules are the most useful. The background area in which the pictorial units will function can be built up from spacing material and furniture. With these units and a press, either a letterpress proofing press or a platen press, it is possible to produce very rapidly a large number of modular designs. This ability to produce a whole series of designs is most important because it is by comparing designs based on different systems of proportion that some evaluation of their relative potentialities is possible.

When starting such a series of experiments it is first necessary to make a decision on the module, in this case the size of type to be used. In this choice, the size of the press bed and the type sizes actually available will be determining factors. In the interests of simplicity it is probably best to keep to one size of type and multiples of one particular unit in that size throughout the design; for example, 6 pt or 12 pt 1 em square border units or face rules cut to multiples of 1 em.

Experiment 1

PROGRAMME

    a Design set in 6 pt, using face rules cut to size and appropriate spacing material.

    b Systematization, pictorial elements of varying length but equal width arranged

FIG 5   Modular setting

horizontally (as in the conventional setting of lines of type).
c Module unit, 6 pt em.
d Proportional relationships based on two Fibonacci sequences. For the horizontal relationships, series A 3 : 5 : 8 : 13 : 21. For the vertical relationships, series B 4 : 6 : 10 : 16. In this initial experiment, in order to express the quality of the relationships as clearly as possible, the natural order of the sequences is maintained. The horizontal intervals working up the sequence 3 : 5 : 8 : 13 : 21. The vertical intervals working down the sequence 16 : 10 : 6 : 4.

TECHNICAL MEANS
The rules were cut from 6 pt Monotype face rules, spaced with 1 em spaces, interlinear spacing by means of lightweight alloy furniture. The setting was made in a galley, the lines parallel to its length and held in place with magnetic quoins. In figure 5 the design is set, in figure 6 the design was first printed in the centre of a square piece of paper, the paper then turned so that the right-hand edge was held in the gripper and reprinted. This produced an interlocking pattern with both vertical and horizontal units and a closer relating of the two series of proportions. Further experiments would be to print the image, then either move the galley 6 pts across the press bed or move the side lay (register stop) 6 pt to the left or right, then reprint. This has the effect of doubling the thickness of all the pictorial elements and of modifying the interlinear spacing. Or, print the image, then reprint it inverted in a different colour. There are endless permutations of reregistration and colour arrangement possible with any such setting: it can also be printed in combination with other type-set images or the same units can be reset in a freer or more complex configuration.

Experiment 2
In this rather more complex experiment the proportional sequence is also used in its

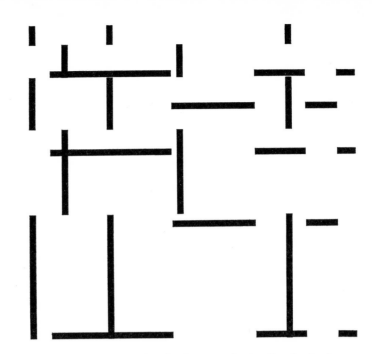

FIG 6   Modular setting
modified

natural order, the single line pattern is also very simple; its complexity lies in the interlinear relationships and the rhythmic patterns developed by their relationship over a
number of groups of lines. In this experiment, a number of initial decisions were made,
the final result of which could not be accurately predicted. It was rather like program-
ming a computer, in fact the end result had a close visual affinity to certain kinds of
computer communication record cards, also various kinds of scientific data records and
printed electronic circuits. The fairly strong movement to the left which develops towards the bottom, breaking across and confusing the planned right-hand movement,
was not anticipated. Nor was the degree to which a very simple arrangement of elements
repeated with a slight but planned interruption would produce such a strong organic
feeling.

PROGRAMME
a Design set in 6 pt using Monotype border units and appropriate spacing material.
b Systematization, pictorial elements multiples of 1 em square border units.
c Module 1 em.
d Proportional relationship.
  Linear spacing, Fibonacci sequence 4 : 6 : 10.
  Interlinear spacing, simple multiples of module unit.
  Pictorial element, simple multiples of module unit.
e Arrangement. Groups of four lines, the first group having a single unit pictorial
  element, one unit being added for each successive group. The interlinear spacing
  of the first group of lines, four units, then diminishing by one unit for each successive group. The arrangement of lines in each group determined by the spacing of
  the pictorial elements, A : B : A : C representing linear spacings of 4 : 6 : 4 : 10.
  The design was intended to become denser towards the bottom and to flow towards
  the right, from a left-hand base line. To prevent the flow being too pronounced an

23

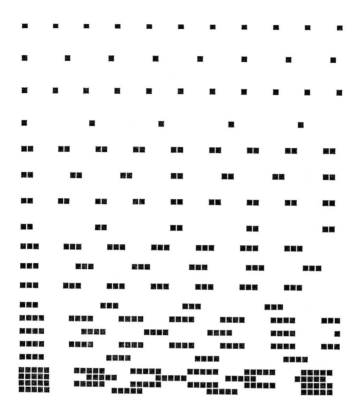

FIG 7   Modular setting

interruption was introduced in the form of a repetition of the first line in each group A : B : A : C (see figure 7).

Further experiments with the same setting

a The image first printed, then reprinted inverted (see figure 8). This gives symmetry on the diagonals, cancels out the downward and right-hand movement, and substitutes a whole series of complementary movements.

b The image first printed, then overprinted with the previous image (see figure 9) at right angles to it. This produces a certain directional stability by balancing the vertical against the horizontal movements and interrupting the diagonal ones, nevertheless the feeling of general stability is lessened by the sharp changes of scale and direction which create a great deal of localized movement and fluctuation.

c The image is printed, then reprinted 1 em to the left or to the right, this makes the whole design denser as one unit will be added to each pictorial element in the design.

The next step would be towards a much freer use of the module, possibly without reference to a specific system of proportions. The image might be based on word patterns such as the interpretation of poetry, either in the form of a visual parallel or in combination with the printed word. Music might also be explored in rather the same way; being particularly modular and mathematical, music of a kind has been produced on a computer.

24

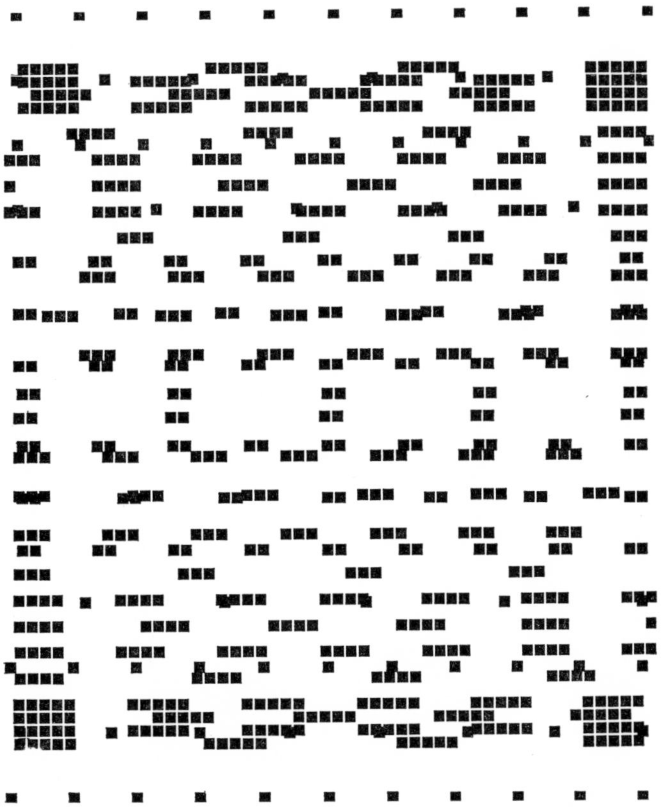

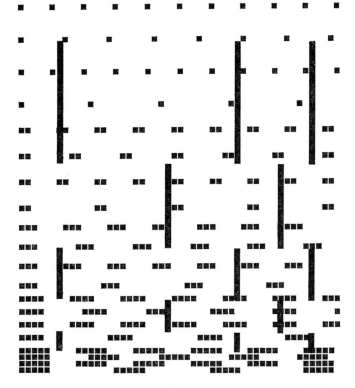

FIG 8   Modular setting,
modification 'a'

FIG 9   Modular setting,
modification 'b'

Other ready-made modular systems

Teaching aids for mathematics, children's bricks and construction kits are often composed of modular units. It is necessary to choose a system having units of a uniform thickness and made of materials sufficiently robust to withstand pressure exerted during printing. Where the units are made of wood there is no problem, but as many are made of hollow plastic and are fairly fragile, care must be taken not to break or deform them. Each system will have a logic of its own, the proportional relationship between the pieces must be worked out and a grid made as a base on which to design. 'Lego' is a good example of a modular construction toy and is based on two modules: the length of each piece is in multiples of $\frac{5}{8}$ inch and the width in multiples of $\frac{3}{8}$ inch (these measurements refer to the sides of the pieces that can be printed from). This system has an advantage in that the pieces can be locked together and built up into larger more complex units.

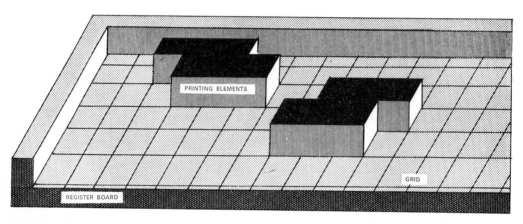

FIG 10   Method for printing from plastic blocks from a toy construction kit

Method of assembly and printing

Figure 10 illustrates the basic assembly of the units. The base board is made of plastic or hardboard painted with gloss paint with the appropriate modular grid scratched into it – this grid provides the method of spacing the printing units. The units to be printed can be temporarily fixed in place on the base board (to facilitate inking up and so on) with short strips of double-sided Sellotape (Scotch tape); they can then easily be detached from the shiny surface of the plastic or gloss painted base board without damaging it and be quickly rearranged as necessary. Strips of wood the same thickness as the printing elements (or a fraction thinner) should be attached round the edge of the base board to prevent them being crushed under excessive pressure. As most ordinary letterpress proofing presses are designed to print at standard type height it is probably best to use a platen press for printing. The various elements in a design can either be rolled up separately in different colours then assembled on the base board and printed from, or first assembled on the base board and rolled up and printed. Register marks can be made on the wooden outer frame of the base board.

A very simple modular exercise is a development of Le Corbusier's 'panel exercise'. In this case the modular pieces are not based on an existing, pre-made unit, but on a system of measurement, a Fibonacci series developed from a module of six feet (72 inches), the average height of a man.

$\frac{1}{2}''$: $1''$: $1\frac{1}{2}''$: $2\frac{1}{2}''$: $4''$: $6\frac{1}{2}''$: $10\frac{1}{2}''$: $17''$

1·5 : 2·4 : 3·9 : 6·3 : 10·2 : 16·5 : 26·7 : 43·2 mm.

Scales of measurements can also be based on other number sequences.

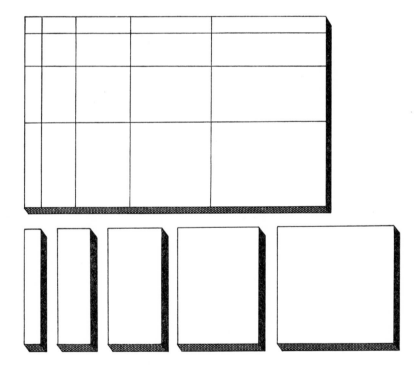

FIG 11 A series of modular rectangles marked out, then cut from board

Working method

Mark out the chosen scale of proportion along two adjacent sides of a piece of thick cardboard or millboard, draw out a grid from these (see figure 11) and cut the pieces out; this can be done on a board or card cutter and it must be done as accurately as

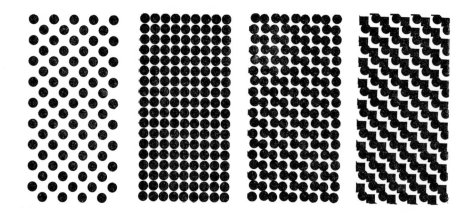

FIG 12   Basic setting of border units and variations produced by reprinting

possible, otherwise the pieces will not fit together or align correctly when arranged in various configurations. The series of modular rectangles produced can be rolled up in ink, arranged on a base board and printed from. They can be used in the same way as described in the preceding section, the pieces being rolled up in ink and arranged on a base board with an appropriate grid marked out on it and printed, or keeping closer to Le Corbusier's 'panel exercise', they can be rolled up in different coloured inks and arranged to fill a predetermined rectangle (based on the same system of proportions) and printed. By rearrangement and reprinting within the same rectangle a large number of permutations of the basic arrangement can soon be produced.

Modular exploration of visual phenomena
In the area of modular exploration we have now reached, several aspects of basic design start to coalesce. The module becomes a tool for examining a wide range of visual phenomena rather than a means of organization and rationalization. The context of its operation becomes wider, more fluid and less easy to define. Up to this point we have been concerned with modular systems of proportion. Modular structures are, however, not only found in association with definable proportional systems. For instance, quite different laws – laws both physical and biological – determine the overall arrangement of such modular structures as the dot formation in a half-tone reproduction or the number of cells and the space they fill of a honeycomb. The eye itself is a most notable biological modular structure, containing over one hundred million light receptor cells (rods and cones) each able to respond to a single photon of light (the module unit of light) at any given time. We have also mainly been concerned with a module as a unit of measurement. It may also be a unit of shape, a square, circle, hexagon, or a structural unit in a geodesic space frame, a transistor in a computer, a scale on a snake's skin or a unit of pattern, check, polka dot, cross or any abstract geometric pattern unit. The American flag, stars and stripes, is distinctly modular but reflecting a social-political law rather than a mathematical-geometric one.

28

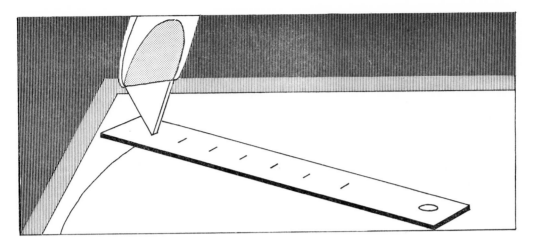

FIG 13 A device for cutting circles from paper or cardboard

TECHNICAL MEANS

1 *Modular dot patterns (set from typographical material)*

Dot patterns can be set up in 12 pt, square or round Monotype border units; an area about 10 inches by 10 inches (25 × 25 cm.) is convenient. A flexible basic arrangement is to set the first line, using 12 pt round or square units alternating with 1 em spaces, with the second line set the same but with the printing units aligned with the spaces in the line above, and so on until an area 10 inches by 10 inches is set. Although no inter-linear spacing is used, there will in fact be a small space between the lines of circles or squares, as they are for technical reasons slightly smaller than the body size they are cast on (see figure 12). This arrangement can be quickly modified by first printing the image then reregistering so that the dots fall into the spaces (see figure 12), giving a much denser pattern. The setting itself can also be altered by 12 pt leading between the lines, and further modified by moving alternate lines 1 em to produce a rectangular dot pattern. By printing in various registrations the circular and square dot patterns can be combined. Other effects can be produced by printing in various degrees out of register and at different angles. This will of course blur the modular quality of the design and produce irrational but nevertheless very exciting effects of movement and optical illusion (see figure 12).

2 *Modular strip patterns built up in wood*

A surface to print a striped pattern can be made by gluing $\frac{3}{16}$ inch (5 cm.) or other sized square sectioned hardwood to a base board of plywood or hardboard.

Paper masking technique can be used in conjunction with the techniques just described to modify and control the image printed from them. The masks take the form of simple geometric shapes cut from paper and laid over the rolled-up printing surface. Apart from circles most geometric shapes are easy to cut out. A series of concentric circles can be cut from up to four sheets of paper simultaneously by using a strip of thick card with a drawing pin pushed through at one end to form a compass centre, and slots cut at various intervals in its length to take the blade of a knife or scalpel (see figure 13).

29

FIG 14   FIG 15

FIGS 14–15   Experiments in optical disturbance

The first two techniques print modular fields of pattern. They can, by various alterations in setting, registration, and combination, produce a wide range of such fields which can be cut up, arranged and assembled in the form of collage, or paper masks can be laid over the inked printing surface and designs made in that way or both techniques can be combined.

Modular fields

Although apparently simple, these modular fields have many unexpected characteristics connected with the mechanics of vision and perception. There is, for example, a tendency for a pattern to alter before the eyes – to resolve itself at one moment into a series of vertical columns or horizontal lines and the next into diagonal lines, crosses or squares. This continual change – the dissolving of one pattern into another – results in a strong feeling of movement. It is caused by the brain trying to rationalize what appears to be, and is in fact, a featureless area of dots signifying nothing or at least nothing of practical importance. Optical illusions of this kind, the feeling of movement, instability, change, with its implied time element, can be intensified in various ways, particularly by the realignment of selected areas of dots or slight alterations of their direction.

3   *Experiments in optical disturbance*

a There is a tendency for a square field of dots to resolve itself into a pattern of

30

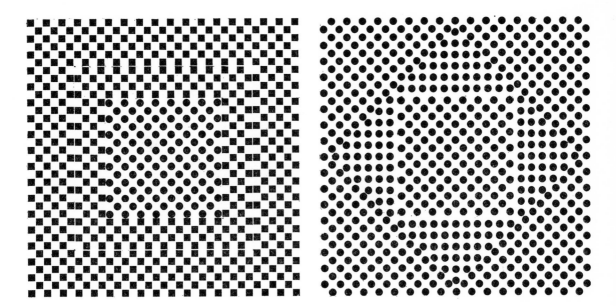

FIG 16   FIG 17

FIGS 16–17 Experiments in optical disturbance

concentric squares, reflecting its square format. This illusion can be enhanced by cutting out a square of the same pattern, and placing it in the centre of the field but in a different alignment. Rather than clarifying the situation, as one might expect, this makes it even more difficult for the brain to rationalize; at one moment the effect is of three dimensions, the next of several overlapping squares or rectangles (see figure 14).

b A similar experiment but with the central square placed at a slight angle to the background field. In this arrangement the edges of the central square seem to alter and fluctuate backwards and forwards from one angle to another, almost as if there were several squares superimposed on one another at slightly different angles (see figure 15).

c In this experiment, the central square is placed on the diagonal of the background field. With this arrangement the pattern of the central square tends to resolve itself into vertical and horizontal lines, the background into diagonal lines; the effect of this diagonal stress on the centre is to distort its linear pattern so that the lines appear to curve or splay out as they approach the junction of the two areas (see figure 16).

Experiment d (figure 17) is basically the same as the preceding ones in method and intention but is rather more complicated.

Striped pattern printed from relief block
modified by masking; two printings (see plates 9 and 10).

1 A collage of rubbings from found objects and
   fabricated surfaces; printed by lithography in
   three printings.

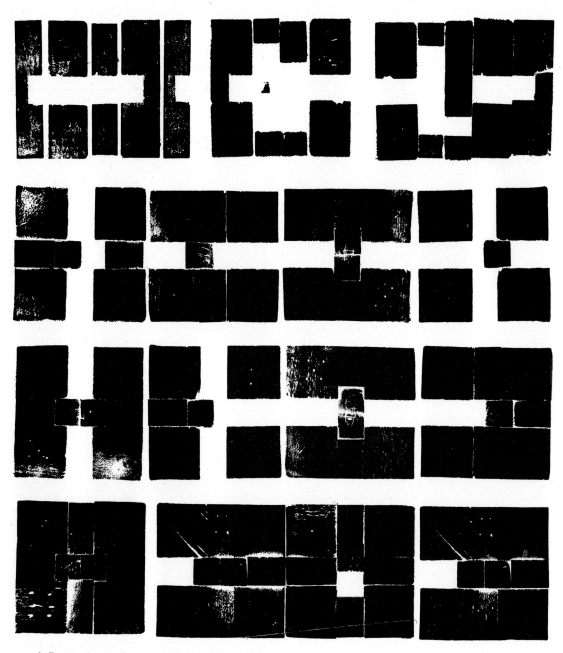

2 A Japanese puzzle, in the form of a wooden
cube; printed at various stages in assembly.

3 A collage of 'rubbings', using the roller
technique described on page 12; printed by
lithography in one printing.

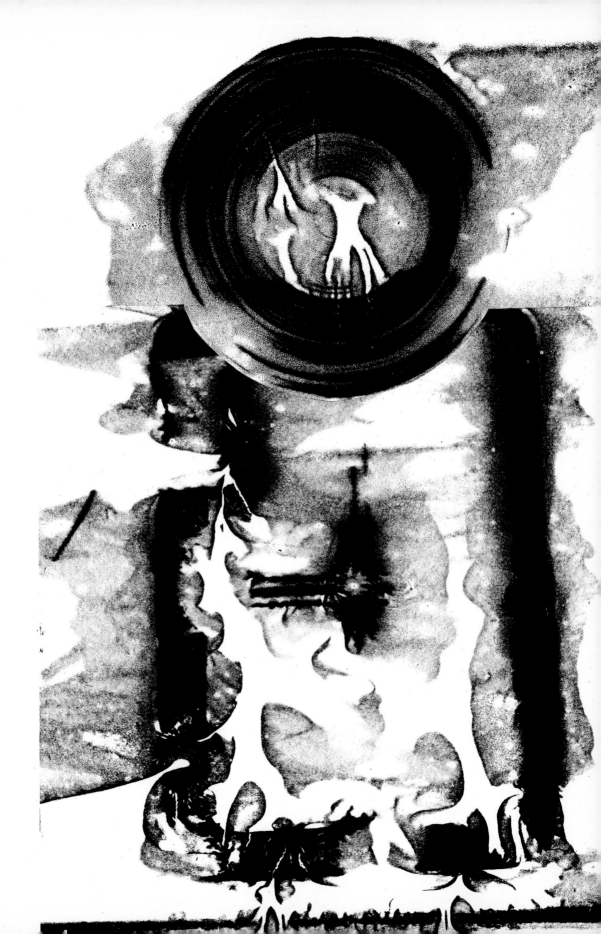

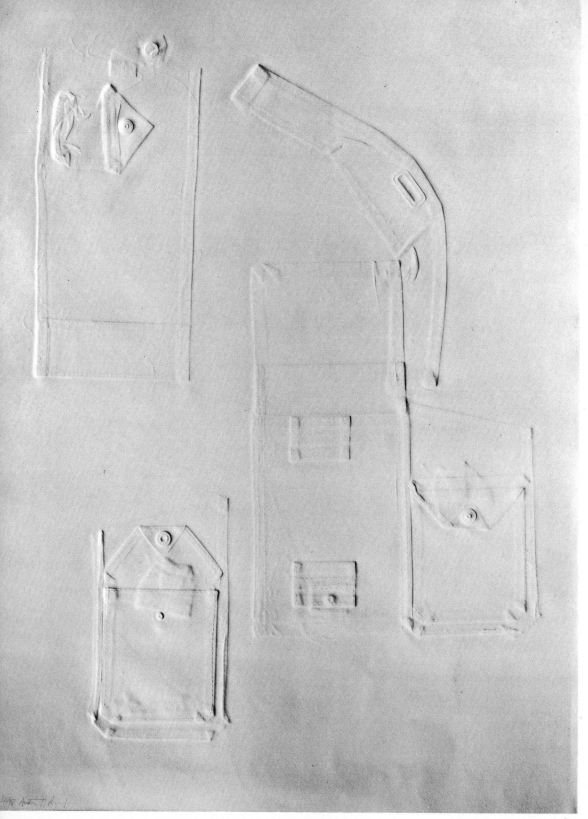

4 Uninked relief print taken from a 'found object'.

5 A collage of 'rubbings', using the roller technique; printed by lithography in one printing.

6   Composition using modular fields to create
optical disturbance, printed from relief blocks in
conjunction with paper masks; three printings.

7   Interference patterns, linear geometric against
random organic, printed from a relief block in
conjunction with paper masks; two printings.

9   Striped pattern printed from relief block
modified by circular paper masks; two printings.

8   Modular field, contrasted with random organic
pattern, printed from Monotype border units,
perforated zinc and paper masks; three printings.

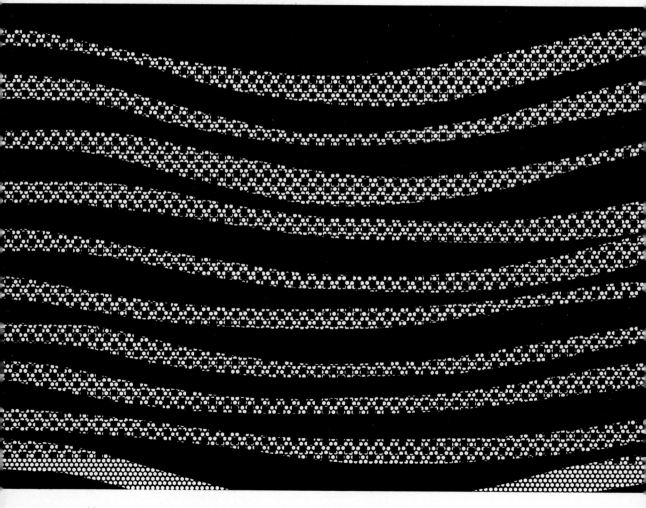

41

10 Circular and striped motifs contrasted, printed
from a relief block modified by masking; two
printings.

11　Optical pattern, printed from a relief block
modified by masking with strips of paper; two
printings.

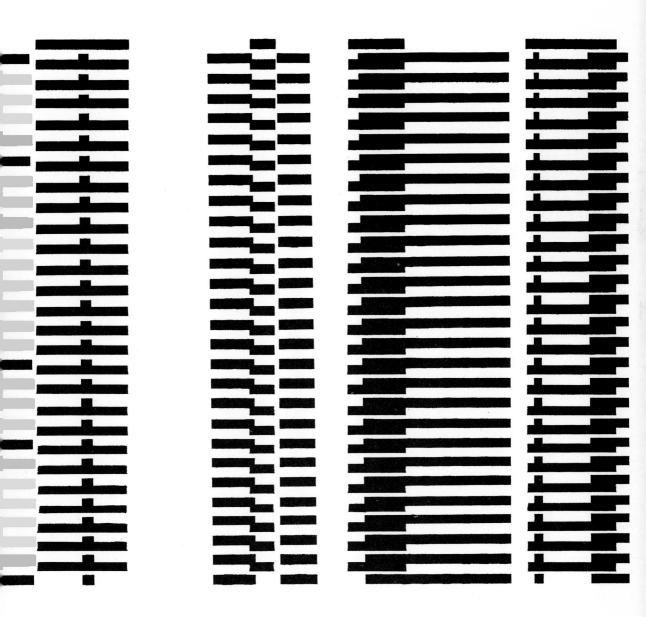

13 Experiment exploiting 'chance'; printed by lithography.

12 Permutation of complex modular units, printed from the back of slugs from a line casting machine; printed letterpress in one printing.

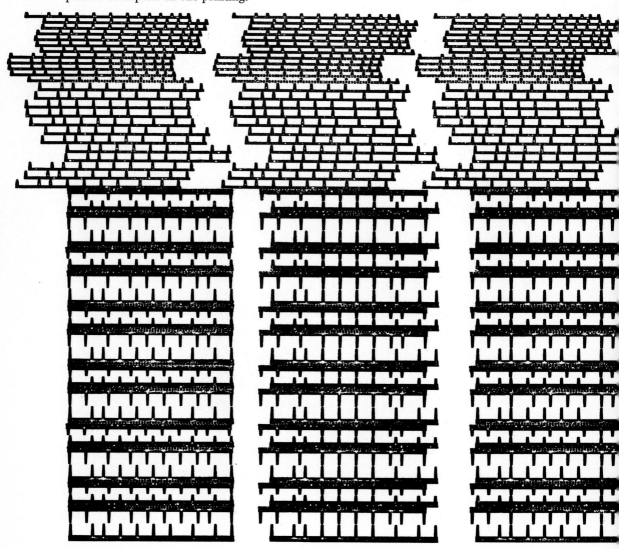

14   Triangles arranged to give a vertical stress;
printed by laying triangles cut from paper onto a
sheet of metal rolled up in ink.

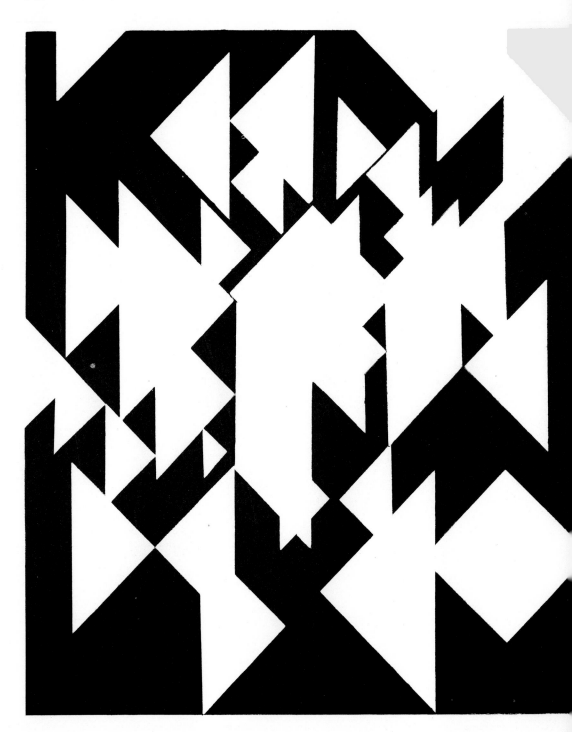

15 Triangles arranged to give a diagonal stress, technique same as in plate 14.

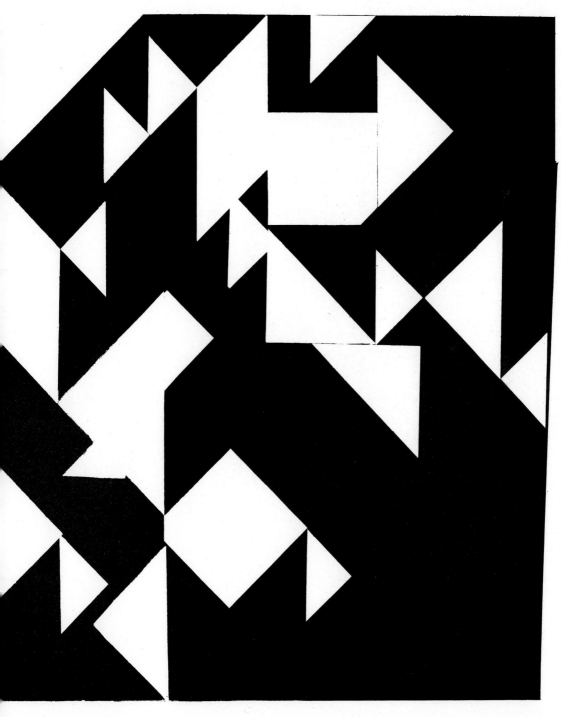

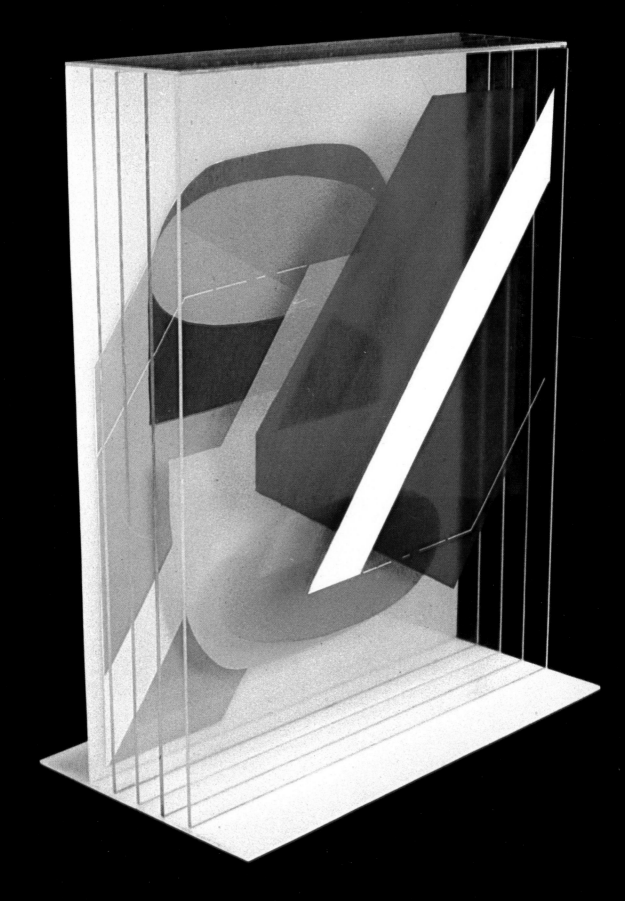

3 Chance and the irrational

In the preceding section we have been concerned with systems of logical arrangement and measurement, with organizational methods for controlling design, with the imposition of order on chaos. Here we are concerned with more or less the opposite, with chance, with the unpredictable, the irrational, with images in which the minimum of particularized control is exercised, with examining the qualities and potential of random arrangements, with accepting and incorporating unconscious forces and in setting up experimental situations in which the 'laws of chance' can operate.

The conscious use of chance in art goes back at least to Leonardo da Vinci, with his reading of figurative images in stains on walls; also to the eighteenth-century English artist Cozens, who deliberately made random blotches of colour on paper, then developed them into romantic landscapes. More recently, Marcel Duchamp produced his series of 'irrational standards' known as *Three standard stoppages* (1913), in which a piece of thread one metre long held horizontally one metre above a canvas was allowed to fall freely onto it and then glued into place; this process was repeated three times. From these records of a particular chance event, templates were made and used in the design of various later works. Jean Arp has also invoked unconscious forces in a number of his collage and reliefs such as *Squares arranged according to the laws of chance* (1916) and *Objects arranged according to the laws of chance* (1930). In these works, pieces of paper or wood were dropped onto a surface and then fixed into the positions in which chance and gravity caused them to fall.

The element of chance can be introduced in a work consciously as a means of determining the form that a particular aspect of it will take. It may be the method for deciding the overall arrangement of the pictorial elements which are themselves calculated geometric shapes. Or it may be the pictorial elements that are the result of exploiting a chance procedure. If, for example, a collage were to be composed of torn pieces of paper allowed to fall onto a rectangular canvas, and then glued into place, the paper chosen and the dimensions of the canvas would tend to be a matter of conscious choice; the size and shape of the pieces of paper would be controlled, but to a more limited extent, by the person tearing them, whereas the method employed to decide on the arrangement of them would embody the highest degree of chance. So we have several different degrees of control involved in the creation of a single image.

16 Three-dimensional structure; printed on Perspex sheets by offset lithography.

Experiments

a Cut a rectangular sheet of cardboard into ten random pieces.

b Shuffle the pieces and then pick one at random, roll it up in ink and take a print.

c Find a piece that adjoins it, roll up the two pieces, assemble them in their correct order on the press and take a print on a second piece of paper.

d Adding a piece at a time (rather in the way a jig-saw puzzle is assembled) take a print of each new configuration until the rectangle has been re-assembled.

The end result will be a series of related, random images reflecting both chance and organic growth. A chain of images, in fact, growing from an arbitrary point through a series of unpredictable configurations to a predictable conclusion.

An alternative experiment is to first shuffle the pieces then 'deal' them out into three piles; roll these groups of pieces up in three different colours. Assemble to form the rectangle on the bed of the press and take a print. The configuration will be the result of the same kind of chance selection of units as that which takes place before a game of cards when the cards are shuffled and dealt. Both these experiments exploit the same kind of contrived random principle of selection as one finds in many games of chance. It is interesting to compare the two distinctly different kinds of image that result from the application of the two programmes of random selection to the arrangement of the same basic units.

Another series of experiments is based on the method employed by Jean Arp to create accidental juxtapositions of elements in a composition.

a Cut a set of arbitrary shapes from plywood or cardboard. The plywood shapes can be cut out with a fret-saw or jig-saw.

b Roll them up in transparent, coloured printing ink.

c Drop them to form a random pattern on the bed of a platen press and take a print.

d Roll the set of shapes up in a different colour or a different tone of the same colour, drop them again on the press bed to form a random pattern and overprint onto the first arrangement.

The image will now consist of two superimposed, disordered arrangements, arbitrarily related, but composed of two identical sets of units. This repetition of units provides an ordering element in a programme otherwise committed to the vagaries of chance. Another version of this experiment is to drop the set of shapes onto a base board and glue them into position, then print, and overprint, altering the registration by some method, such as merely dropping the printed sheet onto the block. Alternatively, torn strips of paper might be dropped onto the inked block and a print taken: the disruption of an already random arrangement, chance modified by chance.

Such situations can be explored in a different way by lithography. Firstly a basic image has to be made, in this case ink splashed, dripped or applied in a series of blind, semi-coordinated gestures would be appropriate. A series of prints are taken of this basic image. Next a print of it is taken on everdamp transfer paper. This is cut up into squares, the pieces mixed up, then reassembled, glued to a sheet of paper with water soluble glue and transferred to a plate in the usual way. This second image can now be overprinted on the first in a different colour; as in the previous experiment chance is modified by chance. In this case, the organic unity of the initial series of random gestures is disrupted by dissection, dispersal and reassembly in a new configuration. The very method used to disrupt has inherent elements of order, however, for by cutting the image into squares, then reassembling it, a rectilinear grid reveals itself in the new image. It is in the overall planning of these experiments that many significant and exciting ideas develop, ideas about the balance and interplay between the rational and irrational. The integration of the aleatory and precisely planned in one work is perhaps most clearly exemplified in Marcel Duchamp's *The bride stripped bare by her bachelors even.* In this work 'canned chance' in the form of the 'three standard stoppages' is absorbed into a most sophisticated system of perspective projections. Just as the 'stoppages' are the means of recording the irrational aspect of the visual world so systems of perspective are a means of giving expression to the underlying order in it.

As the object of the preceding experiments is to explore and comprehend something of the nature of chance it is necessary to cede a measure of direct control. One must be prepared to be not only an originator but also a spectator, to accept the discipline of the accident.

4 Movement, cinetic and kinetic

One of the greatest differences between the world of today and that of the past is the increasing tempo of movement (and consequently of life) and the enormous proliferation of structures which incorporate movement in one form or another; 'speed is basic to our life or relationships. Pressured by continuous dynamic impulses, surrounded by an incessant tide of motion, we have become dominated by this new dimension' (Gillo Dorfles). The truth of this statement is borne in on us with urgent insistence in cities and towns with the presence around us of ceaseless motion, of movement untrammelled by dimension or even material, for this movement takes place as much in the air above us as in the earth below. Above, the jet aeroplane, the helicopter or monorail, beneath, the underground railway: tubes, conduits and wires channelling liquids, gases and electrical impulses.

Around us move the bus, motorcar or motorcycle. Even within the walls of buildings lifts and escalators speed up and down. It is not only in the sphere of communication that one is conscious of this overwhelming tide of motion, it spreads to every aspect of our life. Our very first act of the day may be to use an electric razor or toothbrush, our place of work will be full of machines utilizing movement to perform tasks however particularized or limited – the capstan lathe, mill or automated assembly line, the collating machine or computer, rotary press or typesetter; in the home the washing machine and vacuum cleaner and after work, the television, pinball table or bowling alley (the skittles replaced in their ideal geometric order automatically) and at night the flashing lights of the advertising signs or flicker of the drive-in cinema. Among the first artists to react in a concrete and articulate way to these pressures, this increasing tempo of life, were the Futurists. 'Everything moves, everything runs, everything evolves rapidly. A figure is never static before us, it incessantly appears and disappears. Thanks to the persistence of the image on the retina, things in movement multiply, are deformed and follow one another like vibrations in the space through which they pass.' Apart from the dynamic evocation of a world of total flux this quotation (from the Futurists' technical manifesto) gives a clue to the means they often employed to simulate movement; it was the application of the principles of the stroboscope and the cinema film. Applied in a static format it took the form of a series of graphic registrations of a series of momentarily arrested images. This method, and methods akin to it, were used not only by the Italian Futurists: Boccioni, Carra, Russolo, Balla (the method is well exemplified in *Study of Paths of Movement* and *Abstract Velocity*, both painted in 1913) but also by artists working in Russia and France: Kasimir Malevitch (*The Knife Grinder* 1912), Marcel Duchamp (*Nude Descending the Staircase* 1912), and Naum Gabo (*Drawing for a Kinetic Sculpture* 1915, an interesting work in which techniques developed to portray in static form an actual time event have been used to describe an imaginary or projected one).

There is, however, beyond this obvious movement of machines, a far more subtle movement, one which is largely unseen and unperceived. 'The subject matter of science is change' (E J Kijksterhuis). Electrons spin round neutrons, cells divide, multiply and re-form into more complex organisms, the organisms decay, elementary particles decay, solids change to liquids and liquids to gases, heat is generated by friction, by expansion. Our hearts beat, photons of light strike our retina, messages course along nerves to our brain, the seasons come and go, the world orbits the sun, light reaches us from long defunct stars.

Types and qualities of movement

Rotate, oscillate, explode, implode, surge, slide, swerve, swoop, rise, descend, roll, pitch, yaw, sheer, veer, meander, reciprocate, dive, plummet, orbit, concentric, fractional, vibrate, disintegrate, decay, accelerate, hover, flow, spurt, drift.

Vocabulary of two-dimensional movements

Linear in a horizontal or vertical direction, rotation round a centre located either within or outside the object, repetition, rhythmic beat.

Methods of producing the illusion of movement in a static two-dimensional format

Printing provides two technical devices that can be exploited to give the illusion of movement. First there is the serial nature of its particular function which is to produce a number of identical images, by a process of repetition. This in itself is a space-time phenomenon and is therefore significant in this context. Secondly there is its facility of controlled registration and reregistration, the ability to relate accurately two or more images to one another according to a predetermined plan, and to be able to repeat this procedure at will.

TECHNICAL MEANS
(Registration)

In lithography a development of the ordinary cross-register can be used, by extending the stroke of the register cross parallel to the edge of the plate or stone, and repeating at set intervals along its length the cross stroke. This method of registration can be modified to form a co-ordinate grid round the edges of the plate (see figure 18). This arrangement makes possible controlled movement in a vertical or horizontal direction. Assuming that the grid is marked out in equal divisions (it may be marked out as a progression) to produce a series of identical movements of the image, it can also be used loosely, as a reference for irregular ones. Circular and pendulum movements can be controlled by means of a pin register. A pin is pushed through the print (in the appropriate place) and into the stone or plate (to form a small depression into which it can be located for each reprinting) to form a centre round which the image on the paper can be revolved (see

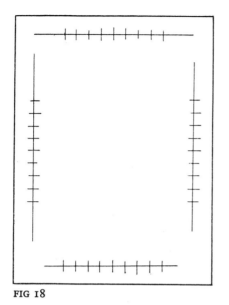

FIG 18

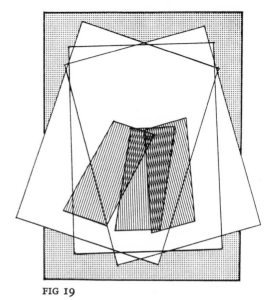

FIG 19

FIGS 18–19   Methods of registration to control movement

figure 19). Similar arrangements can be used in screen printing by marking a grid out on the printing or impression bed for vertical and horizontal movements. For circular movements the print can be revolved round a pin registered against a point on the bed. To prevent ink setting off onto the litho plate or back of the screen (when a number of prints are taken wet onto wet) the print can be dusted with magnesium between each printing.

In relief printing, the 'open block' system can be used, the registration of the paper remaining constant and the printing element itself moved. The degree of movement can be controlled and movements in any direction catered for by marking out the path and phases of the movements required on a piece of paper and fixing this to the register board with Sellotape. A register board can be made by glueing pieces of card to a plywood or hardboard base board to form side and front lays (see figure 20). The movements through which the printing (pictorial) elements are to be taken can be first worked out by laying them on a sheet of paper (of a size suitable to fit the register board) then drawing round them, to record each phase of the intended movement. This is then fixed to the register board, the various elements to be printed inked up, placed in position and printed; they are then re-rolled up, placed in the next position of the phase of the movement and printed in register with the first printing and so on until the print is completed (see figure 20).

The simplest effects of movement are produced by printing and then reprinting the same image several times but in different registrations. The path of the apparent movement is determined by the direction in which either the paper or the printing elements are moved for reregistration. Initially, printing should be done in one colour, a transparent mid-grey is probably best, because its neutrality precludes to a certain extent any psychological overtones or figurative associations. Its transparency enables each phase in the movement to be identified, thus expressing at the same time its continuity.

54

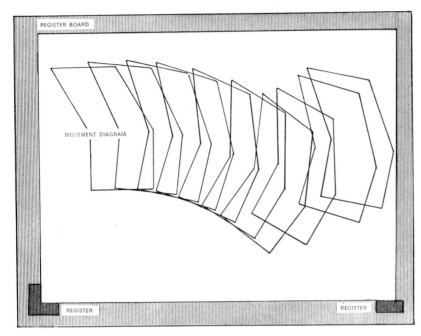

FIG 20   Movement diagram fixed to register board

Experiments

a A sequence of equal movements along a horizontal path.

b A sequence of equal movements along a vertical path.

c The intervals in registration modified to simulate acceleration and deceleration. Extending the intervals between reregistration suggests acceleration, contracting them suggests deceleration and impact.

d The introduction of colour to suggest variations of speed and velocity. In this context, colour will tend to be subjective, although in the way that the speed of an object creates heat through friction and as heat can be suggested by what are termed warm colours, acceleration can be represented by a progression of colours from cool to warm and vice versa.

e Print a series of strips suggesting horizontal movement, with the climax of the movement at a different point on each strip. Assemble these beneath one another to form a composite movement, a wave of movement.

f Movements about a central point, arcs or complete circles.

g Combine all the preceding simple movements, arrange them to cross or overlap each other.

It will be found that any shape subject to repetition along a given path will evoke a feeling of movement along that path. The apparent velocity of that movement will be modified not only by the intervals at which it is repeated but by the character of the shape involved. This will also modify the quality of its direction; for example, it may appear to flow naturally on its predetermined path, or it may appear to be held forcibly to this path, a path seemingly unnatural to its shape: such is often the case in movements round a centre.

55

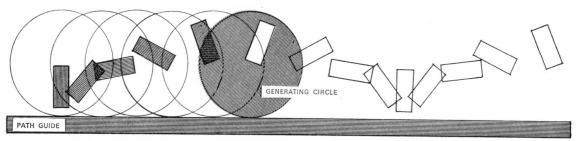

GENERATING CIRCLE

PATH GUIDE

FIG 21   Stencil for cyclic movement

Cyclic movement

TECHNICAL MEANS

A cycloid movement is the combination of linear with circular movement in accordance with geometric laws. Both the 'path' guide and the 'generating circle' can be cut from cardboard of a medium thickness. These are the two basic components for making cyclic movements. The 'path' is a straight strip of card, the 'generating circle' a circle of convenient size cut from the card. This apparatus can be modified to produce movements akin to and derived from the cyclic. For example, the 'path' guide itself can be circular and the generating circle rolled round it, either within it or outside it, or the 'generating circle' itself can paradoxically be square or oval, the movement itself will, however, be basically a circular one. The strip of card forming the 'path' is first fixed temporarily in place on a piece of paper with drawing-pins or rubber solution, the movement is then traced by rolling the 'generating circle' along the path always in contact with it. Care must be taken that it does not slip, otherwise the pattern of the movement will be deformed. To give a controlled degree of movement both the 'path' guide and the 'generating circle' can be calibrated to give a series of equal phases. The shape to be subjected to the movement is cut to form a stencil in the generating circle. This basic apparatus can be used in several ways (see figure 21).

a By merely running a pencil round the stencil aperture in the 'generating circle' and repeating this process through a number of phases of the movement, a diagrammatic drawing of it can be produced. This can be used as the basis for a design, by enlarging significant parts of it, superimposing one part of the phase on another or by combining it with other kinds of movement. The final 'movement diagram' can be used in two ways (1) as the basis for an image to be printed by silk screen or lithography with further development by means of overprinting and reregistration or (2) it can be fixed to a register board, the printing elements cut from cardboard, rolled up in ink and placed in position on it and printed, re-inked and placed in the next position (in accordance with the 'movement diagram') and reprinted.

b It can be used as a conventional stencil, using stencil ink and brush, ink and a soft roller, or even coloured pencils.

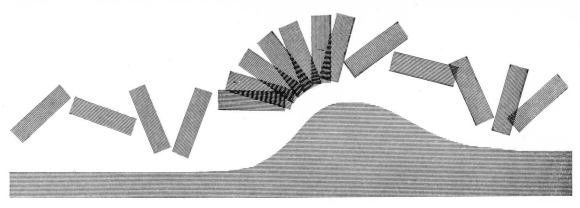

FIG 22   Modified cyclic movement

Cyclic movement and movements derived from it

   a Basic cyclic movement, circle rolling along a straight line with equal movements between intervals.

   b Acceleration and deceleration of basic movement.

   c Two interlocking cyclic movements (two shapes cut from the generating circle on different radii).

   d Two parallel paths, top and bottom; the generating circle rolls clockwise along the bottom guide, moving to the right, then, by still turning clockwise, but in contact with the upper guide, moves (rather paradoxically) left, to give two geometrically interlocked movements.

Having explored some controlled movements, we can continue to explore in two directions; either towards a free, intuitive interpretation or towards further rational, geometric analysis. A step towards freer, less trammelled movement, movements more akin to those in nature, is to introduce a chance element into the scheme, for example a modification of the cyclic movements:

   a Modification of the 'generating circle' to an oval or heart-shape or any irregular shape.

   b Modification of the 'path' of the 'generating circle', introducing random curves (see figure 22).

   c Modification of both 'path' and 'generating circle'.

Or the image can be produced by dripping or splashing ink or paint on a sheet of cardboard and cutting out the shapes to make a stencil of them. The stencil can then be laid on a sheet of paper, a drawing-pin pushed through it (at a point decided by some chance method or intuitively) to provide a centre around which it can be revolved. The stencil can be used in any of the ways previously mentioned. It will produce images in which the various elements will appear to move at different speeds relative to one another. The direction of the arcs along which the various elements travel can be controlled by altering the position of the centre around which movement takes place.

   Controlled movements can be further explored by applying to specific mechanical actions techniques similar to those described earlier in this section. This can be of use (particularly to the graphic designer) as a means of giving visual expression to the characteristic movements of such mechanisms as a watch escapement, or cam mechanism of a line-casting machine.

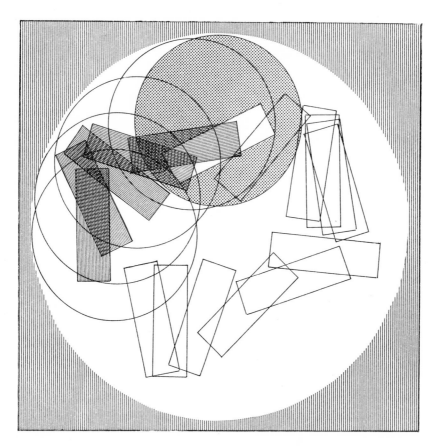

FIG 23
Movement
diagram

Animation of an escapement mechanism

Templates cut in cardboard in the shape of the various parts of the mechanism are assembled and pinned in place (the pins forming the centres around which the various pieces will move) on a piece of paper to form a two-dimensional working model. This 'working' template can be drawn round at various stages in the cycle of movement to produce a diagrammatic record of it. It will be found that careful selection is needed in order to isolate the specific stages of the cycle that are most typical of it and that will give a clear graphic account of its unique characteristics (see plate 22).

The particular quality of the meshing of gear wheels is well described in the 'Technical Manifesto of Futurist Sculpture' by Umberto Boccioni: 'the revolution of two cog wheels with the continuous appearance and disappearance of their square teeth'. Then the combining of the two sets of cogs at their point of 'driving contact', with the apparent disappearance of them at this point and the reappearance of them once this point has been passed, makes a graphic symbol for the dependence of one part of a working mechanical structure on another. At the point at which the teeth of the cogs disappear the two interdependent components become one in their transmission of movement, of power and of energy.

The templates of a mechanism can also be used to print from direct. For this purpose they must be assembled on a drawing board or piece of ½-inch plywood and pinned in place with headless pins. They can then be rolled up in ink and prints taken on a platen press. The assembly can be moved through its cycle of movement and reprinted as desired.

Another interesting mechanism that can be subject to analysis by the same method is the Maltese Cross or Geneva Stop movement. Its interest lies not only in its mechanical ingenuity but in its historical role as the method used to provide intermittent action in various early animation devices such as L S Beal's Choreutoscope of 1866 and also early film projectors including R W Paul's projector of 1896 and L A Le Prince's of 1889.

The effect of movement in a composition can often be enhanced by contrasting the moving element in it with a static one. One part of the image is subject to a sequence of reregistrations, the other is left to form a static yardstick against which the simulated movement can be compared. Two movements can be related so as to activate the space between them, to give a feeling of total flux. Movements ending just short of the edge of a composition suggest deceleration or impact; those continuing across the edge and into the space beyond intimate an endless extension of it.

Another method of giving an account of movement is by a series of static fixes of it, the evolution of the movement or development being unfolded rather as a story unfolds in a strip cartoon, each image being in itself without movement, but forming part of, and being a transitional point in it. Techniques of this kind are used to illustrate such phenomena as the phases of the moon or the growth and evolution of living organisms and so on. A method of printing a series of images exploiting the technique just outlined is by means of a variable printing surface.

TECHNICAL MEANS

The basic apparatus consists of a piece of thick card out of which one or more rows of circles have been cut. The negative section of the card is glued to a firm base and the circles themselves replaced in their respective apertures. As they are not glued in place they may be turned in whichever direction is required. We now have a rigid framework containing a number of adjustable sections, and it is on these sections that the printing elements are glued. These can be in the form of parallel strips, geometric shapes or whatever shape is to be subjected to the series of movements. The whole assembly can be placed on the bed of a platen press, the movable elements rolled up in colour and printed, reset, rolled up in different colours and reprinted (see figure 24).

Motion implied by the passage of time

Time negates order, it disunites, it destroys regularity and symmetry, it disperses, erodes, fragments. Time moves in one direction and is irreversible. An egg is whole and then it is broken – it can never be whole again. If we see the broken egg, we know that

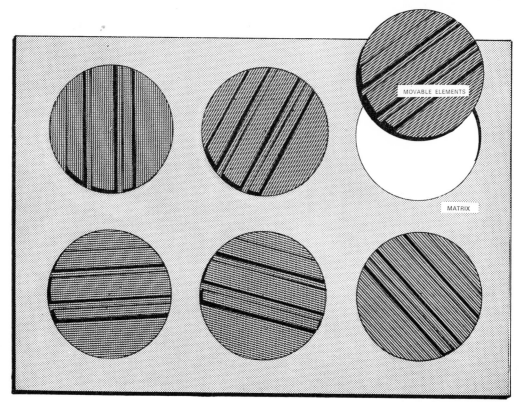

FIG 24   Variable relief printing block

it must once have been complete, it indicates to us that time has passed. So from order to disorder can symbolize for us the passage of time.

Two ways of giving concrete expression to this symbolic means of denoting the passage of time are (a) to start with a formal arrangement of simple geometric shapes, then by a series of rearrangements, each less formal than the preceding one, to arrive at a stage of complete anarchy, or (b) to start with a whole unified shape and by degrees, through a series of stages, break it down until nothing remains. This experiment gives symbolic expression to two qualities of time, that of destroying order and of dispersion and erosion.

TECHNICAL MEANS

a A number of simple geometric shapes are cut from cardboard, thin plywood or millboard; these form the printing elements.

b A grid is marked out on a piece of paper thus giving the initial formal arrangement.

c The printing elements are rolled up in ink, arranged in position on the grid and a print taken.

d The elements are then re-inked and arranged to give the first deviation from the formal arrangement (the first of a series of deviations which will become progressively more pronounced until the original arrangement is completely destroyed). This new arrangement is marked in on the grid (as a reference for the next stage in printing) and a second print taken.

Printing is by means of a platen press or alternatively, as the elements to be printed from are quite thin, an etching press or lithographic transfer press can be used. If printing is done on a litho press plenty of backing, including a sheet of hardboard, should be used to prevent the tympan becoming embossed.

The second experiment can be carried out by silk screen.

a A circle is first cut from a sheet of fairly thin paper. The paper should be a little larger than the printing area of the screen (the area of exposed mesh). This paper stencil is attached to the screen with a few small pieces of double-sided cellulose tape and a print taken in the usual way (once the print has been taken the paper stencil will be held more firmly in place on the screen by the ink).

b A piece of paper torn in a random shape is fixed in position in the circular aperture of the mask (either with double-sided cellulose tape or a dab of ink) and a second print taken. This is the first step in the disintegration of the circle. Pieces of paper are fixed on the screen in a random fashion, and prints taken until the circle is completely obliterated.

Three-dimensional cinetic structures

The continuous re-alignment of elements in a three-dimensional structure, caused by the movement of the spectator in relationship to it, can produce the most complex effects of movement. This feeling of movement is particularly strong if the units of which the structure is composed are built up from simple shapes, such as stripes or circular dots repeated a number of times, so that parallax occurs in many places simultaneously. Such cinetic structures can be built up from sheets of transparent plastic with fields of simple modular elements printed on them.

TECHNICAL MEANS

The image to be printed by offset litho on $\frac{1}{8}$-inch Perspex.

a Set up an area of Monotype border units (see page 29), roll up in chalk-black litho proving ink or transfer ink and print onto everdamp transfer paper, transfer to a litho plate. If the area set of border units is smaller than the area to be printed, as it probably will be, several transfers can be pulled, pasted up to form the area required and then transferred to the plate. If photo litho is available then the Monotype field of dots can be photographed and put down onto a pre-sensitized plate.

b Clamp the plate to the plate bed of a flat bed offset proof press.

c Very carefully set the impression bed to suit the thickness of the Perspex. It is best to have a soft blanket on the transfer cylinder because plastics tend to vary in thickness up to ·015 inch.

d Roll up the plate in plastic or resin-based offset ink, or ordinary offset ink with plenty of cobalt or tinprinter's dryers in it.

e It is not practical to use the paper grippers on the impression bed to hold the Perspex. In any case it does not have to be held down as it is rigid and so will not tend to lift or wrap round the cylinder. Measure out to find the position in which the image will fall on the impression bed, then arrange cardboard lays to locate the Perspex in the correct relationship to it. The lays can be made of fairly thick cardboard and held in position on the surface of the bed with masking tape. The lays should be arranged to locate along the side nearest to the operator and along the right-hand edge of the Perspex; this will prevent it sliding during printing. When printing on plastic with an offset press it is possible to build up the image slowly to the required density (degree of transparency) by taking the work through several times. The printed sheets of Perspex can be arranged in various ways until a satisfactory relationship between them is reached. If it is felt necessary to block out background effects, extraneous to the structure, sheets of opal Perspex can be used; these will give an even diffusion of light. The whole assembly can then be finally glued together using further sheets of Perspex to form a base and other necessary supports.

Kinetic structures

We have so far dealt with techniques for producing the illusion of movement, cinetic art, exploring such phenomena as parallax, where owing to the particular organization of a structure, the fixed relationship between the various parts alter as the spectator moves round it, to produce the illusion of movement. In such structures the spectator provides the physical movement and the structure determines the quality of the movement. Also with optical phenomena, configurations appear that tend to defeat the rationalizing processes of the brain and in so doing create the illusion of movement; for example such as repetition of small shapes at maximum tonal contrast, coupled with ambiguities of direction and contour (see pages 30-1, figures 14, 15, 16, 17). Kinetic structures differ from cinetic ones in that they either move as a whole or parts of them move. This movement is produced either by some mechanical device such as an electric motor, or by such natural motive power as the flow of air or gravity. Some of the earliest works in this field are the *Roto reliefs* (1923) of Marcel Duchamp. These take the form of cardboard discs on which are printed various arrangements of spirals and concentric and eccentric circles. These discs when revolved at a certain speed (they were originally intended to be rotated on the turntable of a gramophone at 78 rpm) give the illusion of movement in three dimensions. The problem involved in exploring movement in this particular way is the difficulty in producing a series of suitable accurate configurations of circles. To produce them by drawing and painting would be both laborious and time consuming. There is, however, a way of rapidly producing a large number of such images by means of paper stencils.

62

TECHNICAL MEANS

   a A number of concentric circles are cut from paper, using the technique described on page 29 (figure 13).

   b A sheet of zinc or plastic etc. is rolled up in printing ink, and the circles arranged on it to form the desired configuration.

   c This assembly is placed on the bed of a lithographic transfer press and a print taken on a sheet of paper, using several sheets of newsprint or a rubber offset blanket, as backing. If the edges of the circles in the print are slightly ragged (this will depend on the thickness of the paper from which the mask is made and the resilience of the backing) the back of the print can be burnished along the edges of the mask; this can be quickly done with the back of the thumb nail. An etching press is also suitable for taking prints in this way. The prints can now be fixed to circular pieces of cardboard and rotated by a small battery-operated electric motor.

The pendulum provides a very simple method of giving movement, it can be used in conjunction with a static image, a revolving one, or with other pendulum movements.

TECHNICAL MEANS

   a Print a field of dots or stripes, by offset, first onto a piece of card or opaque plastic, then onto a piece of transparent plastic.

   b Fix the image printed on the opaque surface to a wall; this will form the static part of the structure.

   c Drill two small holes ($\frac{1}{32}$ inch) in the top corners of the transparent image, then using two pieces of thin nylon or wire, suspend it in front of and about 1 inch to 2 inches away from the fixed image. It should be hung from as great a height as possible, not less than 15 feet, and the two supporting strands must be arranged to hang parallel with each other. It will be found that it will swing for quite a long time if given a slight push.

By combining in different ways pendulum and rotary movements, two- and three-dimensional static images, and images printed on opaque, semi-opaque and transparent surfaces a great range of kinetic effects can be produced. Plastics now come in a wide range of colours including fluorescent colours; certain semi-opaque and light diffusing qualities are also available. Small electric motors designed for driving toys and models can be utilized to provide the necessary motive power, their rotary movement can be converted into other types of movement by utilizing components from such construction kits as Meccano, Philips' Mechanical Engineer, etc. To reduce and control speed it is easier and cheaper to use simple pulley wheels of various sizes driven by elastic belts rather than gear wheels, which have to be very accurately mounted to perform satisfactorily.

5 Colour

Just as solid objects can be described in terms of their three dimensions, height, width and depth, so colour has three basic describable characteristics which are termed the three dimensions of colour. These are hue, tone and saturation.

HUE The pure 'chromatic' colours of the spectrum, having no visual white or black content. Differences of hue are the qualitative differences between colours. Violet, blue, green, yellow etc.

TONE The quality of relative brightness of a colour, the white or black content of a colour. In the terminology of colour mixing and printing the addition of white to a pure chromatic colour gives a tint, the addition of black gives a tone.

SATURATION Chromatic content; the intensity of a particular colour in terms of hue content.

Apart from certain contrived situations, a particular colour will have all these qualities and its character will be determined by the degree to which it has each of these qualities. For example a very light or very dark tone (a tint or tone) of a particular hue will be of low saturation. This phenomenon becomes apparent when actually mixing paint or printing ink; the chromatic content of the mixture must become relatively less as more and more white or black pigment is added. The fusing of the three elements of colour gives what is termed 'colour value', or simply 'colour'. Apart from the intrinsic qualities of a particular colour, colours have certain definite relationships with each other; for example, all colours can be mixed from three colours, called primary colours, red, yellow, blue. For example, red + yellow = orange, giving a natural sequence and analogous colour harmony, red–orange–yellow. If this is carried through we reach a linear relationship red–orange–yellow–green–blue–violet–red. By bending this linear diagram round to form a circle another series of relationships becomes clear, the gradation through from relatively warm to relatively cool hues, giving a warm side and a cool side to the circle. Warm colours advance and cool colours recede, a phenomenon apparent in nature and termed aerial perspective. The relative positions into which colours fall on the 'colour circle' also clarifies one of the most dynamic of all colour relationships, that of complementary colours. These are the colours which appear opposite each other across the axis of the circle. The effect when juxtaposed is to bring out to the maximum their particular character, to intensify or stimulate chromaticity. It is, however, not only the complementary of a particular hue that will modify it; all other colours will to a greater or lesser extent. For example, red will be activated in the following manner:

In juxtaposition with green (its complementary) it will appear purer and brighter
In juxtaposition with blue it will appear yellower and warmer
In juxtaposition with yellow it will appear bluer and cooler
In juxtaposition with black it will appear duller
In juxtaposition with white it will appear lighter and less luminous
In juxtaposition with mid-grey it will appear brighter and sharper.

17 Modular based pattern subjected to a series of
controlled modifications. Theme 'compression';
printed by letterpress.

66

18   Experiment in simulating movement. Theme
'centrifugal force'; printed by stencil.

19   Experiment in simulating movement, four sets
of phases of the same rolling movement; screen
print.

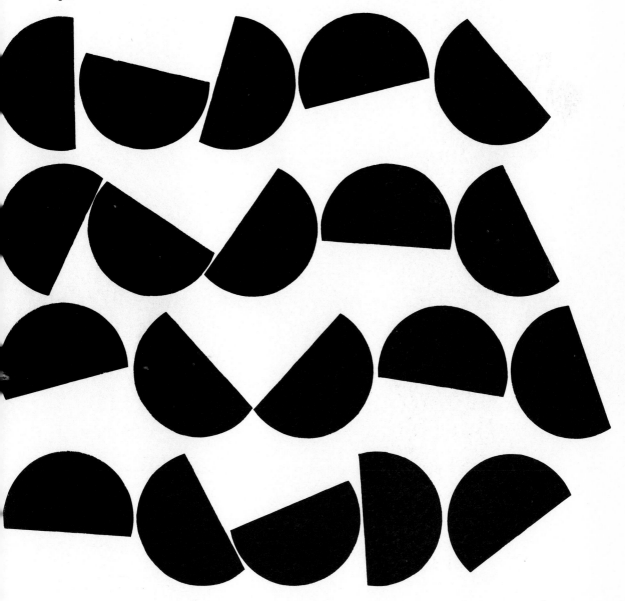

20   Pendulum movement; printed by lithography in three colours.

21 Experiment in simulating movement. Theme
'rolling movement round the perimeter of a circle',
cardboard units, open block relief print.

22 Analysis of 'Geneva stop' movement, using
cardboard templates.

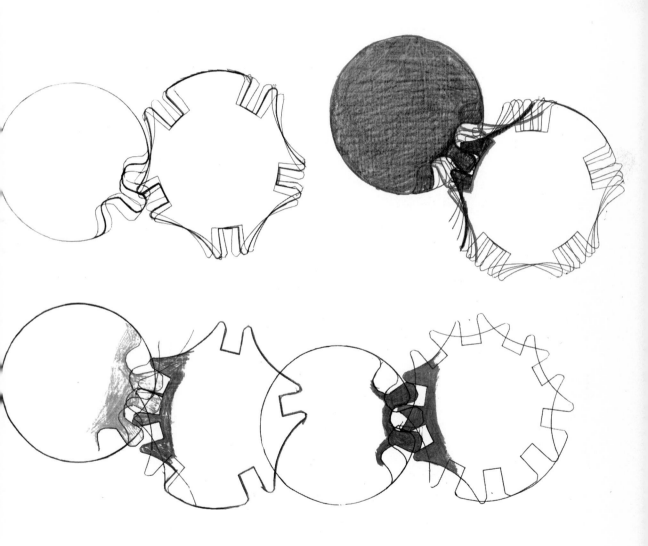

23 Graphic account of the passage of time, order to disorder, cardboard units, open block relief print; two printings.

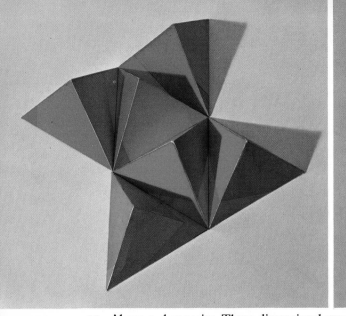

25 Above and opposite. Three-dimensional structure modified by printed surface
configuration, two-dimensional pattern modified by conversion to three-dimensional.

26 Project 1. Theme 'movement'; printed by lithography.

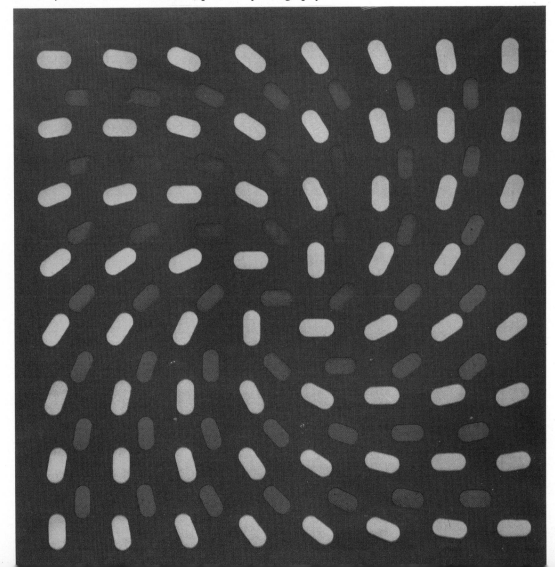

27 Project 1. Basic print modified by overprinting modular field.

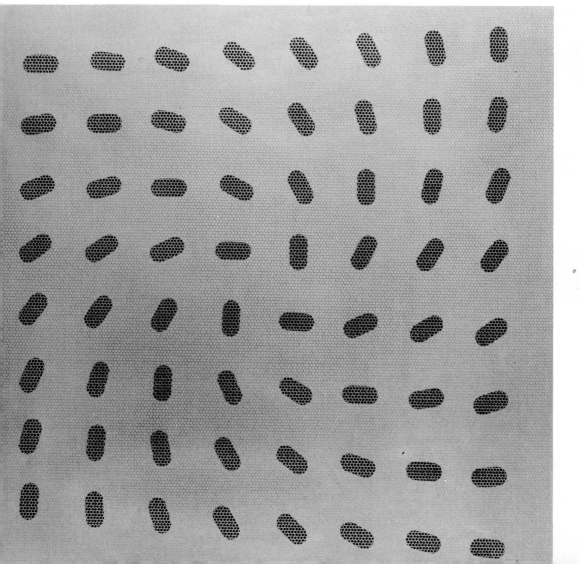

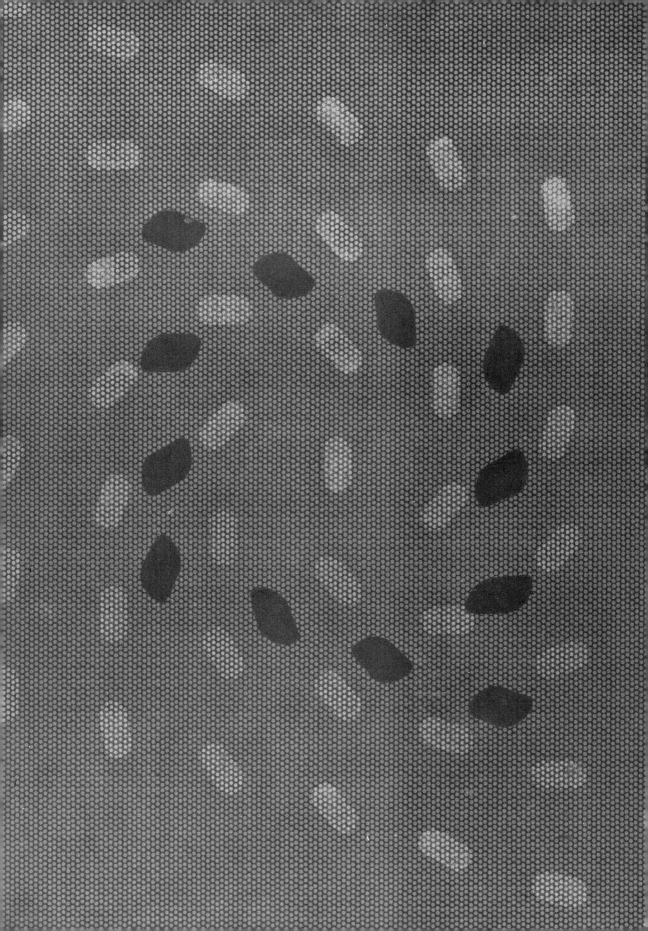

28 Project 1. Modification by distortion, stressing
the diagonal.

29 Circular units projected to form a hemisphere;
printed by lithography.

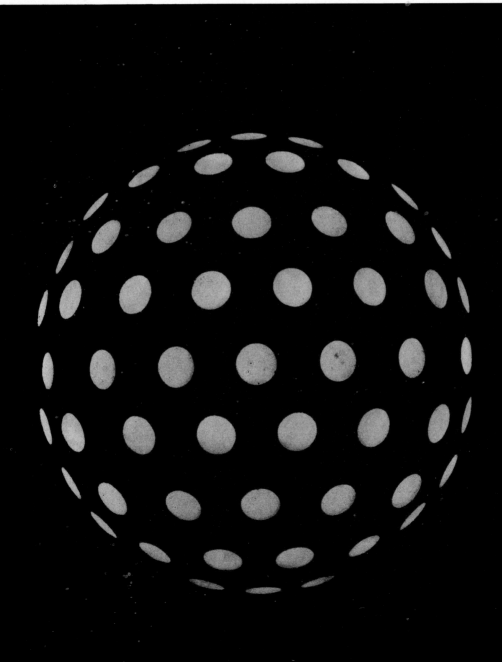

It seemed that out of battle I escaped
Down some profound dull tunnel, long since scooped
Through granites which titanic wars had groined.
Yet also there encumbered sleepers groaned,
Too fast in thought or death to be bestirred.
Then, as I probed them, one sprang up, and stared
With piteous recognition in fixed eyes, hell.
Lifting distressful hands as if to bless. ce was grained;
Yet no blood reached there from the upper ground,
And no guns thumped, or down the flues made moan.
The hopelessness went hunting wild
After the wildest beauty in the world,
Which lies not calm in eyes, or braided hair
But mocks the steady running of the hour,
And if it grieves, grieves richlier than here.
For of my glee might many men have laughed,
And of my weeping something had been left,
Which must die now. I mean the truth untold,
The pity of war, the pity war distilled.
Now men will go content with what we spoiled,
Or, discontent, boil bloody, and be spilled.

30–33 Project 2.
Illustrations to
Wilfred Owen's
poem 'Strange
Meeting', printed
by lithography
modified with paper
masks.

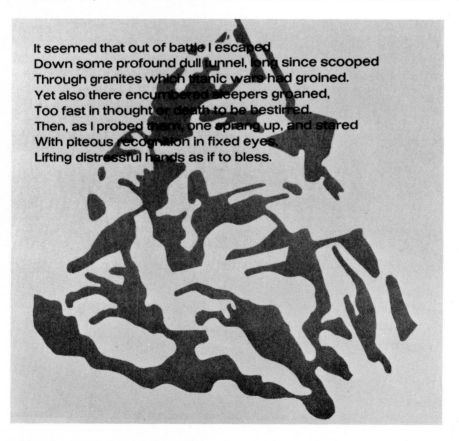

It seemed that out of battle I escaped
Down some profound dull tunnel, long since scooped
Through granites which titanic wars had groined.
Yet also there encumbered sleepers groaned,
Too fast in thought or death to be bestirred.
Then, as I probed them, one sprang up, and stared
With piteous recognition in fixed eyes,
Lifting distressful hands as if to bless.

34 Project 3. Based on a drawing of an aeroplane, printed by lithography modified with paper masks; two printings.

35 Project 3. Image printed then overprinted inverted; two printings.

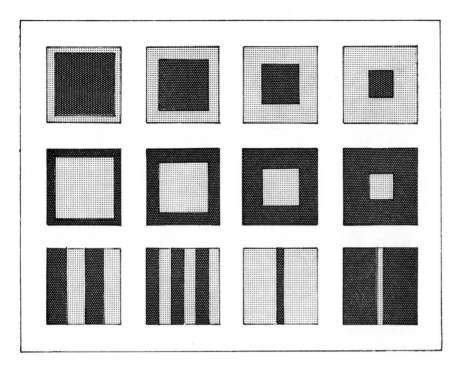

FIG 25   Basic layout for a series of colour experiments

These effects are further modified, particularly in regard to the degree of apparent change, by the tonality and the saturation of the colours involved, also by the relative area and arrangement of them. It will be apparent that in order to understand the effects that are produced by colour relationships it is necessary to experience by experiment a fairly wide range of them. Several conditions must be satisfied in order that such experiments (depending for success as they do on delicate optical illusions) shall be successful.

    a The colour must be laid on as an even film; any suggestions of texture would be alien and detract from the pure effect of colour.

    b The area of the colour should be in the form of a simple geometric shape, and preclude as far as is possible any figurative associations.

    c The edges of the areas of colour must be drawn accurately so that when abutted, colour to colour, no white gaps appear between them, as this would interfere with a true assessment of the relationship.

These conditions make experiments carried out with a brush and poster colour (or similar medium) both arduous and time consuming and certainly preclude a reasonable number of variations of any experiment being attempted. If, however, the areas of colour are printed by lithography, silk screen relief or stencil, a large number of variations in hue, tone or saturation can be rapidly produced, and a number of experiments can be carried out simultaneously. A suitable arrangement for a number of related experiments is shown in figure 25. In the top row different areas of the same colour are arranged

F

against a background of another colour; in the second row the situation is reversed; in the bottom row striped patterns of various densities are used to demonstrate the visual mixing of colour, or patterns to demonstrate figure-ground fluctuations. Such an arrangement would be printed from two plates or blocks. Many similar arrangements are possible, depending on the aspect of colour relationships being studied. Experiments in the visual mixing of colour (the basis of three- and four-colour half-tone printing – examine the coloured prints in this book with a strong magnifying glass) can be made using the same kind of field of dots as that mentioned on page 29. Similar effects can be studied using a sheet of perforated zinc to print from.

TECHNICAL MEANS

For silk screen, the simplest method is to cut a stencil of the shape required from thin, hard, non-absorbent paper such as machine-glazed wrapping paper, using a steel rule and a stencil knife or other sharp knife. Having cut out the stencil, position it on a layout sheet and place the screen over it, dab glue through the screen to hold the stencil in position, then print in the usual way. Alternatively, a heat-adhesive laminated paperback stencil such as 'Profilm' can be used. For litho, the configuration is drawn in lithographic drawing ink onto the plates to be used using a steel rule and a ruling pen. For relief, a cardboard relief block as described on page 89 is the most satisfactory. Simplest of all, an ordinary stencil can be made using a roller to deposit the ink. In each case the edges which abut each other in the two colours must in fact overlap slightly to ensure a clean join. Printing should be carried out in the first instance in opaque colours. If transparent inks are used a thin sliver of a third colour will be produced where the edges of the two colours overlap, even this is preferable in most cases to a strip of white paper.

Although theoretically all pure hues can be mixed from the three primaries, in practice, due to the nature of the pigments available, it is necessary to use at least four colours, for example crimson, vermilion, mid-yellow and blue, plus black and white for modifications in tone and saturation. For the most accurate rendering of the colours, prints should be taken on a good white offset paper. A truly white paper is particularly necessary if transparent colours are being used because the very character of the colour is largely determined by the tone and colour of the paper on which it is printed. The mixing of inks to produce a particular colour is similar to mixing oil paints and acrylic paints. As with oil paints, some colours will be found more transparent than others, for example, vermilions, reds and warm yellows tend to be opaque; magenta, crimson, greens and blues tend to be transparent. Inks are available, particularly for silk screen, in which all colours are opaque. If opaque colours are being used, tints are made by using an opaque white ink such as titanium white. If the colours are to be transparent, tints are made by the addition of reducing medium, the light content of the colour being provided by the paper shining through the transparent film. In studying colour relationships it is not a good

82

idea to keep to mixtures of primary colours only (although a great deal may be learned about colour mixing itself) because in practice very intense colours cannot be produced by mixing two or more colours. For example a magenta composed of say 15% blue pigment and 85% crimson cannot be as intense as one which is 100% magenta pigment.

Surface characteristics of colour

Opacity and transparency have been mentioned only in connection with certain practical problems. The structure and texture of a colour does, however, contribute considerably to its particular character. Colours are often described in terms of their surface character: shiny, matt, velvety, eggshell, opalescent, chalky, translucent, metallic, dull, smooth and so on. Practically speaking there are two basic surface qualities of ink and paint, opaque and transparent; other qualities depend on the way the ink or paint is applied (variations in thickness caused by brush strokes, for example) and the character of the surface it is applied to.

Opaque colour is colour at its simplest; matt, impenetrable, absorbing all light rays except those of the colour itself – ideally a surface devoid of any character beyond that of the colour itself. Such a situation is very rare and such conditions are most nearly fulfilled by distemper or flat undercoating on a smooth plaster wall, or acrylic paint on the smooth side of hardboard. Transparent colour is more complex. It is always influenced by the surface to which it is applied and is characterized by a visual mixing of the film of colour itself and the colour of the background against which it is seen. It is this quality that facilitates colour mixing by overprinting, and is well exemplified in the lithographic printing of flat solid areas of transparent ink on white coated papers.

In painting, transparent colour takes the form of glazing over opaque colours. Apart from the relative opacity or transparency of the ink itself, the quality of the colour is modified by the nature of the ink film and this is determined by the method of printing involved. Lithography, silk screen, relief and stencil printing all print films of ink different in character. For example, due to the thickness of the material from which the screen is made, the film of ink in silk screen printing is much thicker than that of offset lithography which probably prints the thinnest ink film of all the printing mediums.

The surface printed on will affect the character of the colour in two ways. Firstly the degree of absorbency of the paper; at one end of the scale there are the hard sized papers, the cast coated and foil surfaced papers which are non-absorbent: the ink does not penetrate them but forms a hard bright film on the surface. At the other end of the scale are the absorbent papers, hand-made waterleaf papers made in England and Japan, filter and blotting papers; with these the ink sinks in, becomes part of the surface of the paper, giving a semi-transparent slightly matt finish. Secondly there are the mechanical differences in the surface of the paper, the degrees of roughness and smoothness, from sugar paper to smooth offset cartridge papers, antique-finished cover papers to calendered papers. Even the form of the roughness may differ, from laid papers to wove papers, natural finish to embossed.

There is a limit to the contribution that a purely formal study can make to our understanding of the expressive potentialities of colour. It is of all aspects of visual-plastic phenomena, the least susceptible to a useful and meaningful systematization. We tend to understand, to develop an insight into the nature of colour, by being involved in and thus experiencing a number of colour situations. It is a facility provided by print mediums that a number of related, comparative colour situations can be rapidly created. More or less any printable image (that is, an image on a lithographic plate or stone, relief block, or silk screen) can be the starting point for research, by merely printing it in a whole range of colours and tonalities. Something of the interaction between shape and colour can be experienced, shape is modified by colour just as colour is modified by shape. Changes of colour will alter the apparent size, weight, stability and spatial effect of any given shape. Next, a number of contrasting images from hard-edge geometric to tachist, varying in scale, can be printed in the same colour; again the object is to explore the dynamic interaction between colour and shape. In this case the colour is subtly altered and will tend to appear darker, more intense, more vibrant and so on according to its configuration. It is only by comparison that such phenomena can be fully appreciated and it is through printing that such comparative material can be conveniently produced. The combining through overprinting or the printing of various areas of colour in juxtaposition with one another brings us to colour contrast and harmony and the modification of these effects by shape and area. Experiments should be framed to explore such areas as one's own subjective colour preferences, or the possibilities of creating a mood or expressing a sensation through the use of colour; also more easily definable effects such as the creation of space or a feeling of movement, chaos or instability. The same colours used in two different configurations may be found to produce quite different sensations, just as the same configuration printed in different colours and tonalities will create quite different moods. It will be appreciated that when working in this way, endless permutations of colours and shapes are possible and that considerable self discipline is needed if useful results are to be achieved. It is therefore important to define one's objectives with some clarity otherwise there is a danger of being led from one fortuitous effect to another, willy nilly.

6 Projects using basic design methodology

Project 1

The subject of this project was movement: to simulate a movement that radiated out from and described an arc round a common centre, and also to control the apparent speed of this movement by the use of colour.

Firstly the movement was broken down into two separate interrelated components, based on grids of equal density – the direction of the movement to be controlled by the angles of the pictorial elements disposed on the grids; the speed of the movement controlled by the degree of disassociation between the two components to be created by the colours used. Subsequent developments of the image were the use of modular fields in different scales to form static reference grids and rational distortions of the movement; for example, tilting the plane on which the movement takes place.

TECHNICAL MEANS

   a The grids were worked out with the angles of the pictorial elements marked in, in relationship to them, then traced down onto lithographic plates with tracing down paper.

   b A stencil of the basic pictorial element was cut from thin plastic (thin oiled manila could be substituted) and mounted in a small cardboard frame for convenient handling.

   c The pictorial elements were stencilled down onto the plate using a small rubber roller ($\frac{1}{2}$ inch wide) and a mixture of chalk-black proofing and lithographic transfer ink.

   d The plates were processed in the usual way.

Later developments were the superimposition of a modular field of reversed out dots to form both a reference grid and a means of providing a spatial element. This was simply a matter of printing an appropriate area of perforated zinc, by rolling it up in ink and printing on a lithographic transfer press, using plenty of backing. In order to get a really good print from perforated zinc (or plastic, which has rather larger holes) it should be glued down flat to a piece of hardboard or millboard. The controlled distortion of the image was achieved by the following procedure:

   a A print of the image is made on yellow everdamp transfer paper.

   b The image is then cut into strips and rearranged as desired; for example, putting the image into perspective to develop a diagonal-sheering stress.

   c The strips are arranged, glued to a backing sheet of newsprint or similar soft cheap paper with a water soluble paste or glue.

   d Finally the assembly is put down onto a lithographic plate and processed in the usual way for a transferred image. This process can be repeated and further distortions made by cutting up and rearranging the new image.

Project 2

This project was set in the first instance as a 'painting project' for first year DipAD students, with the 1914–18 World War as the subject. From it developed the idea of illustrating a war poem by Wilfred Owen, 'Strange Meeting'.

First the poem was broken down into the groups of lines to be illustrated. The lines were then set up in type and printed on semi-transparent paper, and arranged with the first group of lines at the top of the first page followed by the second group of lines set a little lower on the second page, the procedure continuing on each successive page until, on the last page, a single line appeared at the bottom, thus giving the feeling of a continual forward and downward movement through the book – a movement in time and space, a parallel to the image of the tunnel in the poem 'Down some profound dull tunnel'.

The illustrations were conceived as a series of modifications to the same basic image; that of a soldier lying dead in the churned and rutted mud of the battlefield in Flanders:

> Yet also there encumbered sleepers groaned,
> Too fast in thoughts or death to be bestirred.

The lines of text overlay the image illustrating them. The two are seen together.

Finally there is a recapitulation and the semi-transparent pages of text are reintroduced in a continuous sequence; the text of the whole poem can be seen receding into the distance, losing definition, layer by layer, again symbolizing the tunnel. As the pages are turned, so time passes; one can look to the left (the pages that have been turned) back into the past and, right, on into the future, returning to the time-space conception of the book in expressing the poem.

The basic configuration of the illustration was drawn on two litho plates, and modified to suit the mood of the lines being illustrated; either by printing one or other of the plates, printing them together to form one image, printing in different colours or by printing on various coloured papers also in conjunction with paper masks (see plates 30 and 35) – exploring, in fact, a wide range of colour and combinatorial possibilities. The text was set in Monotype, Univers Bold, 22D on 24 pt and printed on an 'onionskin' airmail paper.

Project 3

The aim of this project was to make a drawn image of an early aeroplane that would convey something of its light, flimsy, almost insect-like quality. The actual aeroplane chosen was in fact a scale model of a byplane in the Science Museum seen against the strong light from a window.

A drawing was first made on the spot and a photograph taken from the same position. The photograph eventually became the basis for the final image. A significant feature of it was the way in which the strong light shining from behind the aeroplane threw it into silhouette and broke through the contours of the wings and struts, giving the feeling that the whole structure was vibrating. To achieve this effect of a form radically modified by light, the negative shapes (those representing the light) were drawn in gum-etch on a lithographic plate to form a stencil and a mixture of washout solution and chalk black litho ink rubbed into the exposed areas to form the image. This basic configuration was printed in black (see plate 34), then a series of modifications were tried with the object of increasing the feeling of stress, lightness, vibration and so on.

a A light grey printing was superimposed over a black print, but registered to form a slight angle with it using the wing roots as a fulcrum. This gave a feeling of wing movement and deflection.

b The image was first printed in grey. The plate was then inked up in black and strips of paper laid across it to mask out a pattern of squares. This black image was then overprinted on the grey one in register. The effect of superimposing the black chequered pattern was to break the image up and increase the rather dazzling, pulsating feeling, enhancing the illusion of light breaking round the structure of the aeroplane.

Another image produced as part of the same project was also based on a photograph taken in the Science Museum. The photograph was of the dark silhouetted shapes of aeroplanes seen partly against windows and partly against a wall and ceiling. The effect was of a complex series of interlocking shadows resolving into several parallel layers and also having a pronounced counterchange motif due to the strong tonal change between the wall and windows. It was decided to resolve the image into three flat areas of tone, and, in order to give a feeling of movement, print one of these areas of tone in mechanical tints. The photograph was first blown up on a Grant projector and the significant areas traced. These were then traced down onto litho plates. The plate with the most extensive tonal area was drawn in negative with gum to form a stencil, and Ben-Day mechanical tints put down at random to form the image. Prints were finally made in various colour schemes and tonal sequences.

7 Methods of printing: with or without a press

Very often the print medium used to achieve a particular effect is not a matter of choice but is dictated by the printing equipment available. It is, therefore, necessary to discover the kinds of image that various items of equipment are capable of printing, irrespective of the particular method for which they were originally designed. The three kinds of printing press most often found in schools and studios are the lithographic transfer press (scraper press), the etching press (roller press) for intaglio printing and the platen press (Albion, Colombian or Washington). Although these presses are all designed for particular methods of printing, they can, if certain precautions are taken, be used to print in other ways. For example, a lithographic transfer press can also be used to print from relief blocks, providing they are thin and of even relief, and from stencils. A platen press can be used to print from a great variety of different objects not designed to be printed from, quite apart from wood cuts and type.

Non lithographic printing using a transfer press
Stencil printing
a Cut a stencil from any reasonably hard, thin, well sized paper.
b Either roll up the bed of the press, or the back of a litho plate or piece of zinc, with fairly soft, direct litho, offset or letterpress ink. The layer of ink should not be too thick (see figure 26).
c Lay the stencil in place on the inked surface, and mask out any unwanted areas of ink round the edge with strips of paper if necessary.
d Lay the printing paper in position and over it lay either six or seven sheets of newsprint or soft paper, or a rubber offset blanket or a thin piece of embroidery felt, plus a piece of backing card.
e Take through the press in the usual way under fairly heavy pressure.
This is a simple, cheap and flexible way of producing a hard edge image.

Relief printing
a Cut the image (the part that is to be printed) from cardboard of a medium thickness, about $\frac{1}{16}$ inch, assemble on a piece of hardboard, the smooth side, and glue into place. A sheet of zinc or aluminium can be substituted for hardboard and if this is the case, when the image is no longer needed, the pieces of card can be soaked or scraped off and the metal used again.
b Roll the block up in ink and place on the bed of the press.
c Lay the printing paper in position and over it lay several sheets of paper plus a sheet of hardboard to prevent the press tympan from being embossed.
d Adjust the pressure and take a print.
This is also a cheap, simple, practical way of producing a hard edge image. If a number of variations of the configuration are required, the cardboard elements that go to make

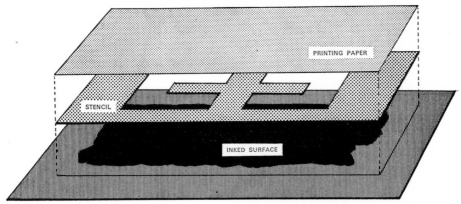

FIG 26 Stencil printing method for use with an etching or lithographic transfer press

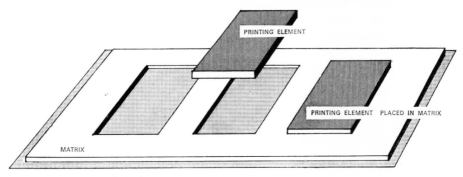

FIG 27 Cardboard relief block

it up can be rolled up separately (in different colours if necessary) then freely arranged on the bed of the press and a print taken.

Printing without a press

Both the methods described have one thing in common: they are very cheap in terms of the materials used to make the printing block or stencil. For making the relief block, almost any kind of cardboard is suitable, and the only tools needed are a sharp knife (a Stanley knife is excellent), a steel rule and two or three small rollers, apart from ink, paper to print on and a press, although even the press can be dispensed with and prints taken by burnishing. If the image is fixed (that is, the cardboard printing elements glued onto a surface), burnishing is quite straightforward and can be carried out in the usual way with a large spoon or small hand roller. If, however, an open block system is being used, the printing elements, as they are so very light, will tend to move during the burnishing and ruin the print. To prevent this happening, lay the elements out in their correct positions on a piece of thin cardboard, mark round them with a pencil, and cut the shapes out. Then roll the printing elements up in ink, locate them in the apertures cut from the card, which forms a matrix to hold them in place while burnishing (see figure 27). This operation must be carried out methodically and with great care. It is made much easier if the ink used is not too stiff and if a hard rubber roller is used for the burnishing.

   In the case of stencils, prints can also be taken by burnishing – either with a spoon or a small hard rubber roller. Whatever tool is chosen as a burnisher, great care must be taken to work round the edges of all the shapes in the stencil, otherwise they will tend to

89

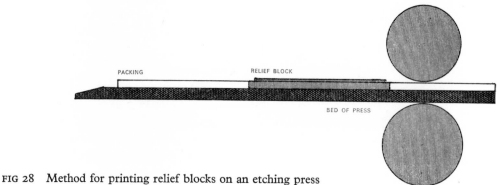

FIG 28   Method for printing relief blocks on an etching press

come out ragged on the print. As with cardboard relief blocks, the materials needed for stencil printing are very cheap and easy to get. Inks (letterpress or offset litho are equally good), paper, rollers, and as a surface to print from use any smooth level surface such as Formica, plate glass, the smooth side of hardboard, sheet zinc or aluminium.

Non intaglio printing on an etching press

Both the preceding techniques can be used in conjunction with an etching press. Paper stencils are printed in the same way as etchings using either etching blankets or a rubber offset blanket as backing. For relief printing the block should be placed on the bed of the press and pieces of hardboard placed at either end of it so that the whole bed is brought up to the same basic height (see figure 28). For backing, a few sheets of newsprint plus a sheet of hardboard or millboard can be used; it is not necessary to use great pressure when printing.

Miscellaneous lithographic processes
Transferring

This is a method by which images made on a specially prepared paper can be put down onto plates.* The most satisfactory paper for general use is yellow everdamp transfer paper. It is possible to draw on it with lithographic ink or chalk to make rubbings or print on it from type or 'found objects'. These images can be cut up, combined and assembled in the form of a collage and then put down on a plate. To put down a transfer, lay a litho plate on the bed of the press, lay the transfer face down on it, then using the usual backing take it through the press under fairly heavy pressure, two or three times. Examine, by carefully lifting one end of the transfer, to see that it has taken on the plate (ideally there should be no black ink left on the transfer paper, only a slight stain). If it has not taken, damp the back of it and take through the press again, repeating this process until the transfer has taken. Then peel off the transfer paper. The plate is now ready to process; additions and erasures should be made at this stage.

Stencilling onto lithographic plates or stones

Images that involve the drawing of small precise hard edge shapes, especially where a particular shape is repeated several times in different positions, are most satisfactorily

*In this section the word plate is used to denote both plates and stones.

90

and easily put onto a plate by means of paper stencils. First trace the position of the various shapes down onto a plate using red chalk tracing-down paper. Cut stencils of the shapes, then, locating them in reference to the tracing on the plate, roll chalk black or lithographic transfer in through them onto the plate with a small roller. When all the shapes have been stencilled down, the plate can be processed in the usual way.

Cardboard stencils (direct method)

One of the simplest ways of printing and one which requires no printing equipment, not even an inking roller, is by stencil. In the stencil techniques so far described the ink is set-off from a flat surface through the apertures in the stencil onto the paper. In the traditional method, the ink is put, by any of a variety of means, directly onto the paper through the stencil (there is no lateral reversal using this system). A drawback of this method is that if the stencil is thin enough to give a hard edge when a roller or stencil brush is used, and if it is of a reasonable size, it tends to be rather frail and difficult to manipulate. It is, however, possible to use a stencil cut from thick rigid cardboard provided the ink used is thinned down almost to the consistency of a dye with white spirit or turpentine, and rubbed down into the paper, through the stencil, with cotton wool. The stencil must be held down firmly and the ink rubbed carefully against the relief of the edges of the apertures in order to produce a hard edge.

Some useful tools and materials

Taking for granted the usual printing materials such as inks, paper, presses etc.
A selection of adhesives: Neogene, emulsion base, or similar acrylic or copolymer adhesive. Grip-Fix, or similar water soluble glue. Bostic 1, other kind of quick-setting adhesive.
Stanley knife, for straightforward heavy work, and a scalpel or craft-tool with a set of different blades for delicate work.
Calibrated steel straight edge.
Sheets of hardboard, possibly cut to a size suitable for the bed of the press being used.
A selection of cardboards of various thicknesses.
Scissors.
A set of narrow rollers, the kind used for rolling up single lines of type.
Some small rubber rollers, $1\frac{1}{2}$ inches by 2 inches wide, the kind sometimes used by house decorators; these are usually quite cheap.
A set of round-hole punches.
A rubber offset blanket, shore hardness 72/76 or the softest available.
Set of drawing instruments.
Double-sided cellulose adhesive tape, Sellotape.
Two very useful pieces of equipment, usually found in art schools, are a light table and a Grant projector, both useful for working out complicated systems of registration.

Sources of supply for printing materials

GREAT BRITAIN

Chemicals and general supplies

Algraphy Ltd
Willowbrook Grove, London SE15

W H Howson Ltd
Ring Road, Seacroft, Leeds 14

Hunter–Penrose–Littlejohn Ltd
109 Farringdon Road, London EC1

Frank Horsell and Co. Ltd
33 Victoria Road, Leeds 11

Selectasine Silk Screens Ltd
22 Bulstrode Street, London W1

Gordon and Gotch Ltd
75–79 Farringdon Street,
London EC4

Screen Process Supplies Ltd
24 Parsons Green Lane,
London SW6

T N Lawrence and Son Ltd
2–4 Bleeding Heart Yard, Greville
Street, Hatton Garden, London EC1

Boots the Chemists
Beeston, Nottingham

Printing ink

Shuck Maclean and Co. Ltd
5, 6 and 7 Ireland Yard, London EC4

A Gilbey and Sons Ltd
Devonshire Road, Colliers Wood,
London SW19

Winstone Ltd
150–152 Clerkenwell Road,
London EC1

Frank Horsell and Co. Ltd
33 Victoria Road, Leeds 11

Lorilleux and Bolton Ltd
Eclipse Works, Ashley Road,
Tottenham, London N17

Paper

Grosvenor Chater and Co. Ltd
68 Cannon Street, London EC4

Spicers Ltd
19 New Bridge Street, London EC4

J Barcham Green Ltd
Hayle Mill, Maidstone, Kent

T N Lawrence and Son Ltd
Bleeding Heart Yard,
Greville Street, London EC1

T H Saunders and Co. Ltd
19 Tudor Street, London EC4

R K Burt and Son
38 Farringdon Street, London EC1

Rollers

Ault and Wiborg
Standen Road, Southfields,
London SW18

Tools

Buck and Ryan Ltd
101 Tottenham Court Road,
London W1

Burgess Products Co. Ltd
Small Tools Division, Sapcote,
Leicester

Presses

G and F Milthorp Ltd
Monkton, Farm Industrial Estate,
Wakefield, Yorks

E G Gallon Ltd
Barkerend Mills, Bradford 3

Advance Machinery Ltd
2 Wine Office Court, Fleet Street,
London EC4

An extremely cheap folding offset
press suitable for the amateur or
secondary schools is manufactured by
Wand Bros, 1 West Street,
Ware, Herts

Chemicals and general supplies

Fuchs and Lang Manufacturing Co.
390 Central Avenue,
East Rutherford, New Jersey

Ault Wiborg Co.
1909 Locust Street, St Louis

Craftools Inc.
1 Industrial Avenue, Woodridge,
New Jersey

Lithographic Chemical and
Supply Co. Inc.
46 Harriet Place, Lynbrook,
Long Island, NY
4227 West 43rd Street, Chicago 32,
Illinois
335 S. Pasadena Avenue, Pasadena,
California

Lithoplate Inc.
5308 Blanch Avenue, Cleveland,
Ohio

William Korn Inc.
260 West Street, New York 10013

Rembrandt Graphic Arts Co. Inc.
River Road, Stockton, New Jersey

NuArc Co. Inc.
4110 West Grand, Chicago, Illinois

George C Miller and Son Inc.
20 West 22nd Street, New York, NY

Printing inks

J H and G B Siebold Inc.
150 Varick Street, New York, NY

Interchemical Corporation, Printing
Inks Division, 179 Albany Street,
Cambridge, Massachusetts

California Ink Co.
2939 East Pico Boulevard,
Los Angeles, California

Fuchs and Lang Co.
390 Central Avenue,
East Rutherford, New Jersey

Paper

R P Andrews Paper Co.
First and H Street, SE,
Washington 3, DC

Japan Paper Company
7 Laight Street, New York,
NY 10013

H Reeve Angel and Co.
9 Bridewell Place, Clifton,
New Jersey

Mead Papers, The Mead
Corporation
200 Park Avenue, New York, NY
Dayton 2, Ohio

Andrews/Nelson/Whitehead
7 Laight Street, New York,
NY 10013

West Virginia Pulp and Paper Co.
230 Park Avenue, New York, NY
35 East Wacker Drive, Chicago,
Illinois
215 Market Street, San Francisco,
California

Rollers

Ideal Roller and Manufacturing
Co. Inc.
21–24 39th Avenue, Long Island
City, NY

Rapid Roller Co. of New Jersey
Fadem and Diamond Roads,
Springfield, NJ

Presses

Charles Brand
82 East 10th Street,
New York 3, NY

Wagner Litho Machinery Co.
555 Lincoln Avenue, Secaucus,
New Jersey

Craftools Inc.
1 Industrial Avenue, Woodridge,
New Jersey

Glossary of English and American terms

BORDER UNITS Decorative typographic units that can be assembled to form borders, but can be used in many other ways

BRAYER Synonymous with hand roller

BRONZE, BRONZING The dusting of a metallic powder ('bronze') onto an image printed in an adhesive to give a metallic effect. The adhesive is usually a special varnish but ink is also satisfactory for this purpose

CARDBOARD Thick board, also other kinds called pasteboard, pulp board, strawboard, mounting board etc.

CHALK BLACK Black, non-drying lithographic proofing ink, having a high grease content

DRAWING PIN Synonymous with thumb tack or push pin in the USA

EVERDAMP TRANSFER PAPER A widely used kind of non-drying transfer paper

FROTTAGE An impression taken by laying a sheet of thin paper over an embossed surface then working across it with a piece of wax chalk or litho crayon. The raised parts of the surface are recorded

GRIPPER The means of holding the paper in register on a letterpress proofing press or a flat-bed lithographic offset press

HARDBOARD A board made from reconstituted wood usually $\frac{1}{8}$ inch to $\frac{1}{4}$ inch thick, sometimes called by a trade name, Masonite

IMPRESSION A print taken from any surface or from a surface specifically designed to be printed from

IMPRESSION BED The paper bed on an offset press

KEY See Register mark

LATERAL REVERSAL The reversal of the image from left to right. The result of direct printing

LAY Means of registration on a letterpress or offset proofing press. There is usually a fixed front lay and an adjustable side lay

LITHOGRAPHIC DRAWING INK Synonymous with lithographic writing ink or Tusche in the USA

LITHOGRAPHIC TRANSFER PRESS Simple, direct lithographic proofing press used mainly in schools and studios. Often called a scraper press in the USA

MILLBOARD A very hard kind of cardboard

OPEN BLOCK The term used to describe a relief block composed of several separate elements, which can be rolled up separately then printed together

PARAFFIN Synonymous with kerosene (USA) a grease solvent used for cleaning inking slabs etc.

'PERSPEX' ICI trade name for poly(methacrylate) sheets; it is similar to 'Plexiglass'. It is an acrylic plastic which is manufactured in either transparent, opaque, semi-opaque or coloured sheets

PLANOGRAPHIC Printing processes in which image formation is due to chemical differences between the printing and non-printing areas of the plate or block and not mechanical ones. In such printing processes, the surface of the plate or block is, for all practical purposes, flat.

PLATE A zinc or aluminium litho plate

PLATE BED The surface to which the plate is clamped on a flat bed offset proofing press

PLATEN PRESS The traditional hand platen press used in schools and studios to print from relief blocks etc. is the Albion and in the USA the Washington or Colombian

PRINTING ELEMENT The part or parts of a printing block or printing assembly that are inked up and printed from. They may be, for example, Monotype border units or merely strips of cardboard

PULLING A TRANSFER Making a print on transfer paper

PUTTING DOWN A TRANSFER Transferring an image from transfer paper to a lithographic plate or stone

'POINT' SIZE Point system of measurement used for type. In the Anglo-American point system 72 pts = 1 inch approximately

REGISTER MARK A mark, usually a small cross, in the margin of a plate or stone to facilitate the registration of successive plates in a colour print

ROLLER Hand inking roller, often called a brayer in USA

ROLL UP To roll up a relief block or litho plate or stone in ink

RUBBING Synonymous with frottage

SELLOTAPE Cellulose adhesive tape; Sellotape and Scotch Tape are both trade names for it

SILK SCREEN Synonymous with serigraphy in USA

SCREEN PRINT A silk screen print or serigraph

TRANSFER INK A lithographic ink formulated for transferring. Re-transfer, type-transfer and plate-to-plate transfer ink are all more or less the same and may all be used for the same work

TRANSFER PAPER A coated paper specially prepared for lithographic transferring

TURPENTINE A grease solvent, used in lithography, etching and screen printing. In the USA 'lithotine' is a non-toxic substitute

WASHOUT SOLUTION Synonymous with asphaltum, used to establish and build up a lithographic image

WHITE SPIRIT A cheap substitute for pure turpentine

YELLOW EVERDAMP PAPER A particular kind of transfer paper

OFFSET or OS Offset lithography; there is no lateral reversal of the print with this method of printing

Bibliography

On Growth and Form
  D'Arcy Wentworth Thompson, Cambridge University Press, London and New York, 1952

The Modulor
  Le Corbusier, Faber and Faber, London, 1954. Harvard UP, Cambridge, USA, 1958

A Guide to Screen Process Printing
  Francis Carr, Vista Books, London, 1961. Dufour Editions, Chester Springs, USA

Linocuts and Woodcuts
  Michael Rothenstein, Studio Vista, London, 1962. Watson-Guptill, New York, 1964

The Thinking Eye
  Paul Klee, Lund Humphries, London, 1962. Wittenborn, New York, 1964

The Art of Colour
  Johannes Ittens, Reinhold, New York, 1962

Colour Technology
  F A Taylor, OUP, London and New York, 1962

A Handbook of Graphic Reproduction Processes
  Felix Brunner, Alec Tiranti, London, 1962. Hastings House, New York, 1962

The Technique of Lithography
  Peter Weaver, B T Batsford, London, 1964. Reinhold, New York, 1964

Basic Design: the Dynamics of Visual Form
  Maurice de Sausmarez, Studio Vista, London, 1964. Reinhold, New York, 1964

Creative Printmaking
  Peter Green, Batsford, London, 1964. Watson-Guptill, New York, 1964

The Nature and Art of Motion
  Edit. Gyorgy Kepes, Studio Vista, London, 1965. Braziller, New York

Eye and Brain: The Psychology of Seeing
  R L Gregory, Weidenfeld and Nicolson, London, 1966. McGraw-Hill, New York

Module, Symmetry, Proportion
  Edit. Gyorgy Kepes, Studio Vista, London, 1966. Braziller, New York, 1966

The Structure of the Universe
  E L Schatzman, Weidenfeld and Nicolson, London, 1966

The Gentle Art of Mathematics
  Dan Pedo, Pelican, London, 1967. Collier, New York, 1959